MONEY TALKS

MONEY TALKS

☞ An Irreverent Guide for the Curious, Penurious, Penny-Wise, and Pound-Foolish

RICHARD SKOLNIK

Illustrations by Aurora Stiffel Berman

CHARLES SCRIBNER'S SONS • NEW YORK

Library of Congress Cataloging-in-Publication Data

Skolnik, Richard.
    Money talks.

    Includes index.
    1. Money—Anecdotes, facetiae, satire, etc.
I. Title.
HG221.3.S57   1986   332.4'0207   86-6469
ISBN 0-684-18623-3

Copyright © 1986 Richard Skolnik

Published simultaneously in Canada by
Collier Macmillan Canada, Inc.
Composition by Westchester Book Composition, Inc., Yorktown Heights, New York
Manufactured by Fairfield Graphics, Fairfield, Pennsylvania
Designed by Mina Greenstein

First Edition

To My Parents,
NATHAN and ROSE SKOLNIK,
who have always made me
feel like a million bucks

2291291

Contents

Introduction

You won't get rich reading this. If you're looking for the way to wealth, put this book aside and continue browsing. You'll undoubtedly find what you want: the shelves groan with volumes offering "practical" "insider" tips and money advice. If you want to know how to benefit from the coming nuclear holocaust, capitalize on creative bankruptcy, or beat the house at blackjack, chances are there's a book on that very subject. On the other hand, if you're fascinated with money—who has it and what it once bought and now can buy—hang on to this book; you will find it to be a celebration of that theme.

What's behind this fascination? Surely nostalgia is part of it. What products and services once cost serve for many as benchmarks in time, poignant reminders of the passing years and of a presumed departure from innocence and simplicity. To give substance to those memories we offer glimpses of the past, at 10-year intervals, at once recreating the era while highlighting what money could then buy. Want to know how far one could go with nickels and dimes "back then" and just how many of them you were likely to earn? You'll get the answers here. But money is more than memories; there's also mystery. About what other subject are people more secretive? What else generates such intense curiosity and endless speculation? Who, for example, is not interested in how much money other people make? In America no other yardstick is quite as important in measuring a person's worth. So we'll apply that measure here and there and observe the particular directions in which cash flows in our society. And once you have money there is no shortage of ways to spend it. Now the question becomes, "What is it going to cost?" Many of the answers we already know. After all, not a day goes by when we are not buying something or other in the marketplace. But there are limits to our purchases, though not to our curiosity about the prices of things. We're interested because price presumes value, and because price determines affordability for us and for others. It's no laughing matter when "they" manage to pay the price and we haven't or can't afford to. Prices also fascinate us because they test our sophistication and savvy and measure our gullibility. "Why pay more?" is a challenge few of us will ignore. When overcharged we feel cheated and exploited and upset at having failed the test of consumer competence.

So we're going to talk money and talk price, consider costs and calculate compensations. All this within some one-hundred fast-paced essays that range widely across the American landscape. There will be lots of money figures to consider, from all manner of sources—personal interviews (e.g., with animal importers and Hollywood managers and vice squad policemen), newspaper and magazine accounts, trade journals, newsletters, price guides, and various statistical sources. Just how accurate and up-to-date are the figures? It depends. Efforts have been made to keep them as fresh and current as possible, reflecting 1985 and early 1986 conditions. But that's not always possible. Figures are collected, figures get processed, and only then are they released. That takes time and so there is a lag. But one must be wary for other reasons. People miscalculate, people exaggerate, people deceive, and about no other subject so much as with money. Why they do is a subject most intriguing, but not one that we need address here. But then, as with other aspects of life, reality is what people believe; truth is of lesser significance. Pronounce an individual worth a billion dollars and few will demur or demand to count his money. Once observe retailers advertising goods "at popular prices" and you'll abandon the idea of objective standards. Perhaps, therefore, it's best and safest to add, as businessmen invariably do, that prices quoted herein may be subject to change without notice.

MONEY TALKS

Adds Up

☞ We live in a market economy. That means it will produce whatever people appear to want or can be induced to buy. The result is an extraordinarily diverse marketplace, one where seemingly insignificant products can enjoy substantial sales. Mark well the figures that follow. You're in for a few surprises.

Some of the weightier figures may not be all that unexpected but their magnitude cannot but impress. Take the $125 billion handed over in 1985 in restaurants, the $50 billion spent on long distance calls, the $25 billion totals for soft drinks. What about our love of candy for which we plunk down $8 billion, or for cookies $4.2 billion, or chewing gum $1.8 billion? When it comes to entertainment the dollars flow liberally as indicated by the annual take for records ($4.3 billion) and movie admissions ($4 billion). Americans love their animals, but a $3.3 billion bill for pet foods? ($2.1 billion for dogs, $1.2 billion for cats.) And there is still $260 million just for cat box filler last year.

Where do some of our food dollars go? A good chunk ($4.1 billion) goes just for cold cereals, $1.5 billion for ready-to-serve orange juice, and $800 million for powdered beverages. The market for chunk light tuna weighs in at $1 billion, while yogurt sales rang up $750 million and frozen pizzas $550 million. For snacks there's always dried fruits ($126 million) and the ever more popular granola bars ($440 million) and dry soup ($438 million). The market for personal care products has never been healthier. We wash up with a bar of soap (a billion dollar a year market), brush our teeth with toothpaste (also a billion dollars), then perhaps swish around some mouthwash ($430 million). Into the shower, where we spent $3 billion on shampoos and conditioners, then it's a shave for the man ($680 million for razor blades) and for all $1.3 billion on deodorants and antiperspirants. After that it's another $450 million on hair sprays and $100 million just for musk fragrances.

Baby's disposable diapers cost us $2.8 billion last year while the figures for facial tissues ($1 billion), bathroom tissue ($2 billion), and paper towels ($1.3 billion) reveal just why reforestation is so important.

If this rapid survey has left you exhausted and slightly dizzy you're entitled to a rest. First, however, recognize that mattresses are a $1.7 billion business (at wholesale) and that the market for water beds and accessories now amounts to $2 billion at retail. Now you can relax, which is yet another market...

Alumni Funds

Bright college years, with pleasure rife, The shortest, gladdest years of life.

AURORA '85

☞ Everyone knows about college expenses these days. The cost of living has moderated in recent years, not so the cost of higher learning. Still sacrifices are made and the bills get paid. Then one day it's graduation and tuition payments end. But don't think you're in the clear. You're now an alumnus and expected to keep up with payments to the college. Now, however, they are called contributions and school spirit becomes the reason for giving. Remembering to do so is no problem. You will be reminded constantly. Schools maintain alumni fund organizations which do just that.

Yale University, to no one's surprise, operates one of the more efficient and successful alumni funds around. Its most recent report glows with satisfaction and features many record performances. Previously laggard classes suddenly perked up and pitched in, endowment contributions increased smartly and portfolio values rose appreciably. Some 44,919 alumni contributed $25.3 million to Yale, both record numbers. That averaged out to more than $500 per contribution, although hundreds of individuals parted with $5000—or $10,000 or more. Class competition was keen especially among those celebrating reunions. Over half the reunion classes (from the fifth to the sixty-fifth reunions) set fundraising records. Leading the way was the Yale class of 1960, now twenty-five years out and in the prime of life and earning power. Some 86 percent of the class contributed a whopping $4.6 million. Never had Yale reaped so bountiful a harvest from any other single class. Those out fifty years, septuagenarians all, came through with a 74 percent level of participation and pitched in with $2.5 million, also a record. But in many ways it was those Yalies back for their thirty-fifth reunion who stole the show. The class of 1950, not previously noted for its zeal, turned born again donors and put $2.2 million into Yale's coffers, a sum twice as large as that contributed by any other class on its thirty-fifth anniversary. Twenty-three classes attained participation levels of 60 percent or better, but recent graduates will obviously require additional cultivation and persuasion. Just 24 percent of the class of 1980 pitched in, a record improved upon just barely by the class of 1975 with a 31 percent level. In contrast 74 percent of the class of 1915 (seventieth reunion) remembered their years in New Haven and those memories were worth money to Yale.

Expressions of satisfaction were everywhere in the report, but there will be no resting on the oars. Nearly 112,000 were solicited in this most recent drive but only 45 percent responded positively. A vast number remain, therefore, to be brought into the fold. Holdouts beware. The Alumni Fund wants you!

Antelopes to Zebras

☞ Remember those movies in which obviously disreputable characters went about the business of capturing, by whatever means possible, noble beasts then offering them for sale in lands far distant? It wasn't that long ago that such practices went on and that animals were spirited across national borders and into the hands of the highest bidders—no questions asked. Those familiar with the field today tell us that's all over with and that the process of animal acquisition proceeds in a thoroughly humane and businesslike way. Of course supply and demand remain the principal determinants of market prices. Tigers, which are easily bred in captivity, are readily available, as are hippos. Zoos can often obtain these just for the asking. It's a different story with certain other species, however. Lowland gorillas don't come cheap. Obtaining one may involve costs upward of $100,000. For several reasons such as decreasing numbers and the difficulty of breeding them in captivity the price of Asian elephants has moved up sharply in recent years. Once available for from $2500 to $3500 each, they'll now come with a price tag of $40,000. Some of the more impressive figures include black rhinos ($35,000), giraffes ($25,000), sable antelopes ($15,000), and gnus ($12,000). Interested in a zebra, figure between $6000 and $10,000 each, a kangaroo, $3000. Of course the purchase price is only the beginning. Animals have to be fed and otherwise maintained. (An elephant consumes $15 to $20 worth of food daily, an antelope $12 to $15.) Once this is all understood you can appreciate why zoo animals must be caged and carefully protected, for outside that cage there lurks that most aggressive and destructive of species, homo sapiens.

Artists at Work

☞ The best time to buy new works of art is probably during a depression. Lots of poor starving artists tend to keep prices low. That's not exactly what motivated the United States government; nevertheless, during the Great Depression of the 1930s it did step in and commission a whole lot of artistic production. Beautification was one of the objectives, but keeping artists from actually starving was of more immediate concern. Putting artists to work was the responsibility of the Federal Art project, an arm of the WPA (Works Progress Administration). It did just that. Enter a public school or library or post office today, one that was around during that era, and you will likely come face to face with murals produced by these artists. Unmistakable are the vigorous, hopeful, vivid characterizations of American themes and experiences. The artists usually were of average skill, but some like Ben Shahn, Willem de Kooning, Jackson Pollock, Charles Alston, and Aaron Bohrod were exceptionally talented. President Franklin D. Roosevelt himself characterized the output as "some of it good, some of it not so good, but all of it native, human, eager and alive." In the end the outpouring was impressive—2,500 murals, 108,000 easel works,

17,700 sculptures, and 11,200 prints. And the total bill for this creative outburst—$35 million. Compare that to some recent government purchases of a couple of ashtrays for $630, two wrench sockets for $800, together with fancy priced coffeemakers.

Bank Robberies

☞ Americans have always had a sneaking admiration for bank robbers, no doubt because bank robbery seemed like a daring, romantic caper and a pretty even match as well, especially when a lone robber confronted a host of tellers, security guards, and a locked vault. Whatever this allure and however rich the tradition of Jesse James, Butch Cassidy, Bonnie and Clyde, Willie Sutton, et al., the fact is that bank robbery as a way of life had come on hard times not too long ago. Indeed it reached a low point in the

1950s when annual robberies numbered only in the hundreds. Not to worry, however. There has been a resurgence. By the 1970s, bank robbery totals were back up to around 2,500 annually and in the 1980s they soared. In 1981 about 7,000 banks came under assault and since that time this figure has hovered around 6,000 annually. But it is not like the good old days. Now the odds weigh heavily against the robbers. Thanks to automatic cameras, bulletproof teller stations (costing about $2000 per station), and rapid police response time (about five minutes), upward of 70 percent of the perpetrators are getting caught. And even if they make good their getaway, their risky labors are not all that well rewarded. Because less money is being left with tellers, the average loss to bank robbers in 1983 was only $6327. For all these reasons the major operators are looking elsewhere for their big scores (for example, armored car holdups are currently receiving more serious consideration). Bank robberies are becoming more and more the province of the amateur and the little guy.

Baseball Cards

☞ At a certain point it was expected that a boy would start collecting baseball cards. Many did, staying with it for a spell before moving on. Some, however, never stopped and it is these "boys" who now form the core group of collectors in what is an expanding market for these picture cards. Outstanding performers on the field have usually become the star performers in the card market. For example, cards bearing the pictures of Mickey Mantle, Willie Mays, Hank Aaron, Ted Williams, and players of that caliber have in recent years consistently commanded high prices. Today you can get a 1955 Topps mint-condition Wally Post for $1.25, but for that same year expect to pay $30 for Jackie Robinson, $60 for Sandy Koufax, and $100 for Roberto Clemente. And, as with all collectibles, some items are simply priced out of sight. That distinction, for example, goes to Honus Wagner cards issued between

1908 and 1911. Find one and you'll be $25,000 richer for it. Settle for Ed Plank in that same series of cards and the bids will start at $5500. Of course prices do fluctuate. Throughout the 1970s the Topps 1952 Mickey Mantle card stirred little excitement, with only about a one-dollar asking price. The 1980s, however, brought an explosion of interest in the former Yankee slugger and the value of the card skyrocketed to $3200 in 1981. Today that interest continues, but you'll only need about $2600 to get one. Four years ago a Pete Rose 1963 card (his rookie year) brought about $55. With Rose breaking Ty Cobb's record in 1985 that same card, in mint condition, rose to $350. So it just may be time for a thoroughgoing cleaning of the junk-filled attic. Uncovering one or two forgotten cards from one's youth could make it all worthwhile.

Quiz Number 1

1. The highest priced slot machines in Las Vegas will accept a silver token worth_____each.
   a) $10   b) $25   c) $5   d) $50

2. Hourly wages of workers are the highest in_____.
   a) Zurich   b) Tokyo   c) Geneva   d) Los Angeles

3. The subway in Mexico City costs_____.
   a) nothing   b) $1.00   c) 14¢   d) 25¢

4. In the 1980 census it cost_____per person to count the American people.
   a) 75¢   b) $1.85   c) $4.75   d) $12.15

5. Operating a commercial hot air-balloon in the air costs about_____an hour.
   a) $175   b) $85   c) $225   d) $550

6. To operate an aircraft carrier (fuel, food, crew pay) for a day costs_____.
   a) $78,000   b) $1.2 million   c) $490,410   d) $173,220

7. Henry Leland's first Cadillac Model A sold for_____.
   a) $1750   b) $1200   c) $1525   d) $2800

8. McDonald's planners anticipate the opening of at least_____stores each year.
   a) 1,100   b) 500   c) 250   d) 800

9. The ABC network paid_____million to cover the 1984 Olympic Games.
   a) 125   b) 185   c) 310   d) 225

10. The US navy budget for fiscal year 1985 was_____ billion.
    a) 62   b) 100.3   c) 185   d) 200

☞ *Answers:* 1) b; 2) d; 3) c; 4) c; 5) d; 6) d; 7) a; 8) b; 9) d; 10) b.

Battle Toll

☞ What is the point of putting a price tag on our wars? After all, we've fought them to defend our nation, prevent aggression, make the world safe for peace loving peoples, and to help freedom, democracy, and justice gain a foothold. What's that worth? But price tags have been attached to all our major military undertakings. So now you can judge for yourself which were worth the costs.

Not until the Civil War did the cost of conflict exceed a billion dollars ($8 billion in this instance). The Mexican War was a steal. (Mexicans would agree.) We sent our fighting men into Mexico, defeated the opposing forces in less than two years, and picked up a sizable chunk of Southwestern territory as the spoils of war— all for a mere $107 million. It cost us more ($124 million) to fight the War of 1812, which was at best a stalemate and entirely without territorial gain. No one would fault us for investing $149 million in the Revolutionary War, not much of a price to pay for independence and nationhood. Costs, however, would have been considerably higher had not the French pitched in, sending money and supplies and troops to ensure the defeat of their old adversaries, the English. "That Splendid Little War," otherwise known as the Spanish-American War is a good example of the escalating price of conflict. It was over in just a few months yet the bill came in for $2.5 billion. Fight outside the country and transport men and equipment all the way over to the Philippines as well as Cuba and it's going to cost you.

The era of inexpensive wars was now over. Despite our belated entry into World War I and the extensive use of Allied equipment, it still wound up costing $66 billion. But no war we had fought quite prepared us for the expenses of World War II. A massive effort was required to equip our men and also supply our allies in the struggle against Germany and Japan. Money was spent like never before in the history of the world. When it was over our direct bill came to $560 billion. Spending billions had now become commonplace. It made it easier to spend $70 billion to bring the

Korean War to an end, but Vietnam would have been hard to swallow at any price ($121.5 billion). Of course all these figures are dwarfed by what our military now spends each year to keep us out of war (more than $300 billion). If this is the cost of peace the next war may in comparison be something of a bargain.

Behind the Stars

☞ Top-level entertainers may perform alone but certainly don't work by themselves. Behind them, out of the public eye, a carefully chosen coterie largely determines career direction, performance schedules, and public image. Few stars would ever consider leaving home without them. First and foremost there is the personal manager charged with plotting those key career decisions upon which stardom often depends. Is it the right time to make a film or will a TV sitcom be the better move? Is Las Vegas the place or will smaller clubs and comedy houses provide a better environment? Making such calls and arranging the deals earns the manager 15 percent of the performer's gross. Scheduling the actual appearances usually involves a booking agency. For 10 percent it will contract for specific dates at Vegas, Atlantic City, Reno, Tahoe, and tie up the loose ends of a TV special or a film project. Once the money starts rolling in, enter the business manager. Bills must be paid, monies sheltered, investments scrutinized, expenses calculated, and earnings distributed. Price tag for such services? Usually 5 percent off the top. But all of this forward momentum could stop. The public, after all, is fickle, styles change, and new faces are always in demand. That's the reason for hiring a public relations agent or firm. Count on it to produce a steady stream of publicity to maintain fan interest and to enhance public image. Ordinarily such favorable attention is available for $2000 to $2500 per month. You may also, if you wish, add the following individuals to your entourage: a road manager responsible for keeping tours running smoothly, a valet, a dresser, or beautician attending to personal needs, and a social secretary orchestrating public appearances and personal commitments. Little wonder then that entertainers don't travel lightly or cheaply. No surprise either that they insist upon top dollar. A Joan Rivers may get $250,000 a week to play Atlantic City, Don Rickles may command $30,000 a show in Las Vegas, a Sinatra, Cosby, Rich Little, Paul Anka, and Rodney Dangerfield will all do just as handsomely; but remember they have lots of mouths to feed. But so long as audiences are entertained the folks behind the scenes will remain well nourished.

Big Bass Bucks

☞ Were anyone to tell you about fortunes to be made underwater your first thought would probably be sunken treasure ships. But such finds are notoriously difficult to come by. Even the fabulous

Atocha discovery uncovered by Mel Fisher's Treasure Salvors Inc. in 1985 represented the fruits of sixteen frustrating years of searching and millions of dollars in expenditures. More reliable and ultimately more rewarding are not old ships but fat fish, bass to be precise. Big-time bass fishing is on its way and lots of folks are gearing up to take advantage. The lure is professional tournaments with payoffs even larger than the proverbial ones that got away. And behind these are the fishing equipment companies casting about for successful anglers to sponsor in return for valuable publicity. The old fishing hole and the traditional fishing derbies are giving way to rigidly supervised events designed for professional fishermen who pay fancy entrance fees and come equipped with boats and electronic gear as sophisticated as that available to naval intelligence forces. For sure, the bass have no idea what they're up against nor any sense of what they may be worth to those folks on the other end of the fishing line. One of the prime movers in the field is the Bass Anglers Sportsmen Society, or BASS, whose top prize back in 1967 (its first tourney)

was $2000 but is now angling to sponsor an event where first place will be worth $136,000. Even before that event, fishermen will have their choice of a number of tournaments (usually involving several days of fishing with prizes awarded for total catch) where the winners will receive $50,000 to $100,000. (Ordinarily the bass are not the losers. After being weighed in they are set free.) In 1985 BASS sponsored contests totaling about $2.5 million. As in every professional sport there is an elite who consistently walk off with the lion's share of the prize money and enjoy annual earnings well into the six figures (tournament prizes plus endorsements). And because big money is at stake, the sport has occasionally attracted those whose efforts have gone not into catching bass but into rigging the outcome. One such ring of cheaters managed to win four tournaments in Texas in 1983 and a total of $244,500 before their scam was uncovered. Without doubt, the big bass mean big bucks today.

A Big Money Year: 1985

☞ You won't find a year-end review of money records elsewhere, so take note of the following healthy figures. While the Dow Jones Industrial Average exploded past 1,500 to a record high, the national debt proved equally energetic en route to the $2 trillion level. Merger mania gripped the corporate world, producing the largest non-oil merger ever, the $6.3 billion deal between General Electric and RCA, and the largest court award in history, $10.5 billion against Texaco for seeking to prevent a proposed Pennzoil-Getty deal. Clint Murchison, Jr., could have used Mel Fisher's luck. While Murchison filed for bankruptcy, in debt to the tune of $400 million, Fisher's search for a sunken seventeenth-century Spanish treasure ship paid off with a find valued at about $400 million. No need to dive for dollars if you had one of the winning tickets in New York's $41 million summer lottery drawing. Even some animals held their own in the year's dollar derby. A yearling brought a world record $13.1 million at a Lexington, Kentucky, auction even though no horse has ever won more than the $6.5 million recorded by John Henry, who was retired in 1985. The money, of course, was in the mating, the reason why a Holstein cow brought a record $1.3 million at a Vermont auction. Political animals didn't do badly either. Books written by Geraldine Ferraro, Tip O'Neill, and Jeanne Kirkpatrick each were sold at auction for about $1 million, while David Stockman tells all for $2 million and historian Edmund Morris for $3 million will sum up the Reagan presidency. If precious political memories were in demand, so were precious objects. An American painting sold for $4 million, a 1913 Liberty nickel for $385,000, a single bottle of wine supposedly ordered by Thomas Jefferson for $156,450 and a Lincoln photo for $104,500, records all. 1985 was a big year for big money.

Bijan

☞ Imagine owning a well-stocked men's clothing store in the high-rent commercial district of New York City and averaging only five or six customers a day. Sounds like the very conditions that lead inexorably to bankruptcy court. Ordinarily so, but not if the store happens to be Bijan and those five or six shoppers are mostly world-class notables who are each likely to put some $25,000 into the till.

There have always been those few proprietors and a handful of establishments that the elite accept as the very essence of high chic exclusivity. Quite often there is a foreign-born owner, an exotic whose very presence suggests cosmopolitanism. And there must be the flamboyance to elevate the shop heads above the rest, suited only for the very rich or those for whom flamboyance is merely a restatement of the familiar. At Bijan the pizzazz is unmistakable, from a $10 million decor featuring luxurious chandeliers, stairways, and tapestries to Mr. Bijan Pakzad's own personal lifestyle, which includes residences in New York, Los Angeles, and

Italy, and an assortment of luxury cars including two Rolls-Royces and a fleet of Ferraris, Aston Martins, and Cadillacs.

Bijan designs the men's clothes featured in his New York and Los Angeles stores. His by-appointment-only customers—who include President Reagan, Frank Sinatra, four kings, and twelve foreign Presidents—are generally not disposed to check price tags first. Neither will they be put off by $400 shirts or $2000 suits or even $150 ties. A $34,000 topcoat, a $9500 suede jacket, and a $120,000 chinchilla bedspread might, however, prompt some second thoughts. Is there anything at Bijan for the common folk? Bijan certainly hopes not, although he is planning to introduce into department stores a version of his men's perfume. It may then be possible for the rest of us, unable to acquire the Bijan look, at least to enjoy the sweet smell of success.

Billionaires

☞ They're quite rare but hardly an endangered species. They represent a new strain, though one clearly related to older stock. To talk of a billionaire some years back was to indulge in fantasy, to exaggerate well beyond known possibilities. According to *Forbes Magazine* we're speaking not of some freaks of finance or a single corporate colossus but of fourteen individuals at work in a variety of areas who each have amassed the phenomenal sum of $1 billion. Of course that total is hardly fixed, changes daily, and is beyond easy verification (or immediate liquidation). A downturn in the financial market, a drop in real estate values, a shudder in the economy, and these billions could turn quickly to mere hundreds of millions. Such matters are not, however, our concern. Our interest is in those fourteen exceptional people.

They're not young. It does take some time to amass fortunes of such magnitude. At forty-eight Leslie Wexner (The Limited apparel shops) is the youngest and four others are in their mid-50s. At seventy-six Harry Helmsley (New York City, real estate) represents the older generation. They tend to have more kids than the rest of us. (All but one are married.) Take away Helmsley, who is childless, and Wexner who is single, and the rest of the group averages four children (none has less than three).

Now you'd think that to pile up that kind of wealth you'd need the flying start provided by a king-sized inheritance. It can happen that way, such as with the two daughters of oil tycoon H. L. Hunt (the only women in this group) or the grandson of John D. Rockefeller, but remarkably, eight of the fourteen did it largely on their own. And while rags would not quite describe the cut of their clothes at the start, six of the eight began with little more than exceptional drive and ambition. Daniel Packard's (Hewlett-Packard) original stake was $595. Henry Ross Perot (Electronic Data Systems) got underway in 1962 with $1000. Leslie Wexner borrowed $5000 from an aunt to finance his entry into the clothing business, while Harry Helmsley entered the real estate business as an office boy at $12 a week.

One of the nice things about our billionaires is their wide geographical distribution. They haven't left themselves vulnerable by clustering in one city or region. Dallas is of course represented (three) and naturally New York City, but you'll find Sam Walton (Wal-Mart Stores) out in Bentonville, Arkansas; John Kluge (Metromedia) in Charlottesville, Virginia; Warren Buffet (Berkshire Hathaway) in Omaha, Nebraska; and Leslie Wexner in Columbus, Ohio. So next time you're in the area perhaps you'll catch sight of one of these most recent products of our ever surprising capitalist system.

Quiz Number 2

1. In 1984_____percent of mothers with children under 6 were in the work force.
   a) 32   b) 52   c) 42   d) 18

2. The product group that commands the most outdoor billboard space is_____.
   a) beer   b) liquor   c) resorts   d) cigarettes

3. The brand that has the largest share of the market is_____.
   a) Mountain Dew b) Diet Pepsi c) Tab d) Dr. Pepper

4. The fine in China for having a second child is_____.
   a) $75   b) $125   c) $1000   d) $350

5. The Warsaw Convention limits the liability of airlines to _____per passenger.
   a) $25,000   b) $125,000   c) $500,000   d) $75,000

6. Movie box office receipts exceeded_____billion in 1984.
   a) 7.2   b) 4   c) 2   d) 9.5

7. In 1984 the Japanese controlled_____percent of U.S. electronics market.
   a) 8   b 25   c) 14   d) 41

8. American women on the average purchase_____new garments each year.
   a) 18   b) 30   c) 38   d) 53

9. In 1984 the market for athletic footwear exceeded_____for the year.
   a) $1 billion b) $4 billion c) $750 million d) $8.1 billion

10. In 1982_____people were prosecuted for nonpayment of federal taxes.
    1) 6,277   b) 1,624   c) 22,004   d) 921

Blockbusters

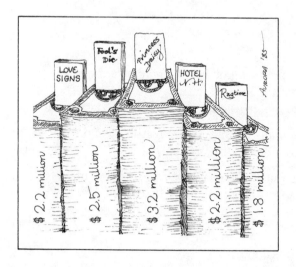

☞ In Hollywood it's the bonanza film that is the stuff of studio celebrations, in the pharmaceutical field, the big drug (perhaps for ulcers or high blood pressure) that sets the industry astir, while in the record business a blockbuster album is the elixir. The same holds true in the book trade.

Every major book publisher needs a runaway bestseller every so often to stay profitable. (The general estimate is that 40,000 new books appear each year.) And for the most part there are but a relative handful of authors likely to write the big books. They are the ones who get the big bucks while the rest of the writing community had better be doing something else between the lines. (A study done a few years back indicated that only 28 percent of full-time writers earned more than $20,000 annually.) The standard payoff for writers involves percentages of the list price of the hardcover edition (usually rising to 15 percent), but the dollars really begin to mount up when publishers bid for the paperback rights. Here are some of the big winners of recent years. The top bid for the paperback rights to Judith Krantz's *Princess Daisy* reached $3.2 million. It climbed to $2.5 million for *Fools Die* by

Mario Puzo and $2.2 million for John Irving's *Hotel New Hampshire*. Both Linda Goodman's *Love Signs* and Erma Bombeck's *Motherhood: The Second Oldest Profession* also topped out at $2.2 million, while E. L. Doctorow's *Ragtime* was settled for $1.8 million. Add to some of these figures payments for book club sales and film and TV movie rights and you're into payoff levels where fact and fiction begin to meet.

Born Too Soon

☞ Suggest that the talents of yesterday's baseball stars exceed those of today's heroes and you'll get an argument. No one, however, will challenge the contention that most of the stars of the past couldn't cash even a month's paycheck of many of today's players. Of course no one back then made $371,000, which is what the average player earned in 1985. Translating actual salaries into today's dollars does help some; but even so ballplayers, whatever their talents, never had it so good. Do the names Dave Kingman ($892,000 a year), Dennis Eckersley ($900,000), André Thornton ($1.1 million), or Sixto Lezcano ($480,000) rank with Willie Mays, Mickey Mantle, Ted Williams, let alone Ty Cobb or Dizzy Dean? Nonetheless all of them are earning more than those old-time superheroes. In fact only a handful of former stars earned (in today's dollars) more than the average player today. Leading the list is Babe Ruth, who in 1985 would have been drawing $576,000 (plus, because of his legendary appetite, all the endorsements currently going to William "The Refrigerator" Perry). Ted Williams would today be earning $423,000 and Joe DiMaggio $408,000, each above the current $371,000 average. On the other hand, you could sign Honus Wagner for $96,000, Tris Speaker for $164,000, Ty Cobb for $301,000, Jackie Robinson for $137,000, Willie Mays for $271,000, and Mickey Mantle for $339,000. It's best to be philosophical about all this. Being good is fine, but being good and lucky to be born at the right time is truly the winning combination.

Brand Loyalties

☞ Unlike sports fans you won't find product managers thrusting a finger into the air to proclaim they are number one. But they're no less proud of what their "team" has done to put their product ahead of the competition. There's pride involved for sure but mostly there are profits. Market share is the name of the game as competing companies battle for a larger slice of the pie. Whether it's soft drinks or network TV ratings, the difference of a percentage point or two can be worth millions of dollars.

Across the 1985 economy there are champions of long standing. Who doesn't know that General Motors (45 percent of the market) is king of the road or that Honda (49.3 percent) wins the race for motorcycle sales? Marlboro leads the cigarette pack with an incredible 21 percent share in an industry where a .5 percent share can be the grounds for satisfaction. Name the world's bestselling packaged cookie? Why it's Nabisco's Oreo cookie, of course. The Ritz cracker, also by Nabisco, has long kept the opposition at bay. Kodak's leading position in amateur color films seems unassailable, while Swanson has a lock on the frozen dinner market. Peanut butter fans will probably recognize Skippy, not Jif or Peter Pan, as the reigning champion while honors in the field of popping corn go to Orville Redenbacher. Who do most people turn to for bandages? Johnson and Johnson of course. For luggage? Samsonite.

Runaways aren't that exciting. Where is the real competition, you ask? There's no shortage of highly competitive markets. All of us have watched Hertz and Avis go at each other for years. Still in the lead is Hertz (33 percent of the market share to 24 percent for Avis). The battle for prime time TV ratings is fierce. Positions change frequently. Current figures show NBC nosing out CBS with ABC lagging behind. Stay tuned for further developments. On the disposable diaper front Kimberly Clark's Huggies cling to a narrow lead over Procter & Gamble's Pampers with Luvs (Procter and Gamble) a distant third. Ragu, which once ran over the opposition in prepared spaghetti sauce, is now facing a serious challenge from newcomer Prego. The soft drink wars go on with the two veteran contenders each too crafty to permit the other to deliver a knockout blow. Current standing has Coke in the lead over Pepsi (21.8 percent to 17 percent) with Diet Coke, 7 Up, and Sprite following well behind. Up in the air it's American Airlines with a narrow lead over United in the battle for domestic flight supremacy. Following in their wake are Eastern, Delta, and TWA. Finally in the great toothpaste wars Crest is currently squeezing out Colgate by a wide margin with Aqua Fresh, Aim, and Closeup getting the brushoff. For all the participants, the competition is fierce, friendless, all consuming. As spectators we can't escape the ads but we can enjoy the show.

Bride Money

☞ They get you coming and going. It can cost plenty to get out of a marriage and, as the following figures reveal, quite a bit to launch one. In 1983 the 1.6 million first marriages generated an estimated $20.1 billion in retail sales. Here's how that adds up: one billion dollars for rings; $2.3 billion for honeymoon travel; $6.2 billion for weddings and receptions; and $10.6 billion for home furnishings. A recent estimate puts the price tag on average weddings at between $4000 and $5000. That there are better investments, ones easier to liquidate, cannot be denied. Still every year close to two million people remain willing to speculate in marriage.

"Joe sent us"

1926

Most of the country's 120 million people in 1926 no doubt led largely prosaic lives, but even they had to sense a new buoyancy on the American scene. On the economic front the signs were unmistakable. Wondrous consumer goods were entering American homes at an accelerating pace. Even in the absence of ready cash, instant gratification was possible thanks to the miracle of immediate credit and installment purchases. America's love affair with the auto grew ever more passionate as the number of cars out on the road climbed steadily. American businessmen proclaimed they had tapped the secret of sustained prosperity and stepped forward, as they had done so often before, as the champions of the American Way, the architects of the new order. Leading the celebration was President Coolidge himself with strong support from Herbert Hoover, his secretary of commerce, and Andrew Mellon, treasury secretary. The forward momentum was everywhere, but nowhere was it as impressive as in Florida where a land-buying spree of major proportions was underway. Surely America was on a roll.

All the cheerleading and self-congratulations couldn't paper over the fact that the new, fast-paced, chic, modern society left many an American baffled. Many of these folk didn't have electricity in their houses; certainly they had no cars at their disposal. They even wondered whether science itself was up to much good, given the kind of new ideas it tended to encourage. These "other" Americans would be heard from. Throughout the year attention remained riveted on a courtroom in Dedham, Massachusetts, where defense lawyers kept up their efforts to gain a new trial for their clients, Nicola Sacco and Bartolomeo Vanzetti, convicted of murder during a robbery attempt back in 1920. Because they were immigrants—and anarchists no less—public opinion showed little sympathy for them or for those who saw them as innocent victims. To most Americans Sacco and Vanzetti were what was wrong with the recent flood of immigrants and precisely why immigration reduction, enacted just a few years earlier, had been the proper remedy.

Similar attitudes were behind the efforts underway in a number of states to remove the teachings of evolution from the schools. The previous year had seen the sensational "monkey trial" in Tennessee of John Scopes, a high school biology teacher arrested for teaching evolution in his class. His conviction encouraged others to insist that evolutionary theory be kept out of the schools because it contradicted the Bible and because it represented the views of scientists, sophisticates, and city people. Other folks, uneasy with the changing world around them, struck back in more dramatic ways. Some gathered into a resurgent Ku Klux Klan to lash out against all manner of perceived threats and enemies. Blacks, Catholics, Jews, foreigners—all were the target of Klan-inspired venom and terror. The Klan was proud of itself, proud of its struggle. This was certainly the impression one received while watching it parade in sheets and hooded masks all through the streets of Washington, D.C., as it did during the year and as it had done in previous years.

No doubt the issue that brought the two Americas face to face in 1926 was Prohibition, since 1919 the law of the land. Many viewed it necessary for the salvation of the nation, but probably just as many found it utterly unacceptable and largely unenforceable. Flouting the law became the standard procedure in many parts of the country. New York's mayor, Jimmy Walker, for example, openly patronized speakeasies, and elsewhere there was a dramatic surge in the number of prescriptions of "medicine" containing alcohol. (In November the US Supreme Court upheld a federal law limiting the prescription of medication with alcoholic content to once every ten days.) Violence surged as Prohibition agents did battle against rum runners and speakeasy joints, while gangster empires such as Al Capone's in Chicago thrived on the control of weapons and whiskey. Was the medicine becoming worse than the disease? More and more Americans were beginning to think so. State referenda held in November confirmed this. Voters in Illinois, New York, and Wisconsin called for repeal of or a substantial modification in the Prohibition laws. In Nevada voters answered "Yes" to the question, "Is Prohibition a failure?"

Had liquor consumption been legal, public toasts would have been in order for a host of individuals who distinguished themselves during the year. It was a time for derring-do and grand exhibitions, a time for stars and the celebration of the famous. Few individuals were more eagerly embraced and accorded celebrity status than Rudolph Valentino; no idol of the silent screen enjoyed a more devoted following than he did. But 1926 was the last year for Valentino. Early on his wife received a final divorce decree against him, then on August 13 he was operated on for appendicitis and a gastric ulcer. Shortly thereafter he died. Scores were injured when over 30,000 devoted fans turned out for his funeral in New York City. His body was then shipped, as he had requested, to Hollywood, California, for final burial.

It was a much better year for George Herman Ruth, outfielder for the New York Yankees. Throughout the baseball season the Babe kept the Yankees ahead of their closet pursuers in the American League, batting an astounding .372 and belting out forty-seven home runs to lead the league. (His closest competition, Al Simmons, had nineteen home runs.) Ruth continued his heroics into the World Series against the Cardinals. In one game he set a World Series mark by smashing three home runs. Still he alone couldn't stop the Cardinals, led by their pitching ace, Grover Cleveland Alexander, from winning the Series four games to three. Still the Babe managed to capture the headlines afterward when he visited Johnny Sylvester, age eleven, in the hospital to thank the youngster for his letter urging him to hit a home run in the Series. Johnny had not been disappointed. The fans of Babe Ruth rarely were.

Hats went off to two pairs of travelers during the year. In May

Lieutenant Commander Richard E. Byrd, USN, and his pilot, Floyd G. Bennett, flew over the North Pole. Then Roald Amundsen, Lincoln Ellsworth, and Umberto Nobile took a different approach. They flew over in a dirigible. Again the public imagination was stirred. There was no less admiration for the success of Edward Evans and Linton Wells. This pair succeeded in going around the world (20,100 miles) in 28 days, 14 hours, and 36 minutes, a record time. Young Gertrude Ederle of New York had her eye on another record. On August 6 this nineteen-year-old became the first woman to swim the English Channel. Fame followed, as did a tumultuous ticker tape parade in New York upon her return. But what of Clemington Corson? The following month this mother from New York City plunged into the Channel heading toward England. She also made it, becoming the second woman, but first mother, to meet the challenge. There was confetti aplenty for Mrs. Corson upon her return to New York City.

Sports history was made on September 23 when over 125,732 spectators paid $1,895,727 to watch Gene Tunney, twenty-six, battle Jack Dempsey, thirty, for the heavyweight crown. The fight had been staged by that most able of promoters, Tex Rickard, who couldn't have been happier as he surveyed the immense crowd and calculated what would be record gate receipts. Unfortunately, the spectacle took place amidst a heavy downpour. In the end Tunney was the victor. The new champ pocketed $200,000. Dempsey could not have been disappointed with his share, some $700,000.

Johnny Weissmuller, Bobby Jones, Walter Hagen, Bill Tilden— there were plenty of outstanding sports personalities around as well as other legendary characters. Some were fallen heroes such as Charles Ponzi, indicted in Florida for a series of fraudulent schemes. He had long been regarded as something of a financial wizard. There was Aimee Semple McPherson, to some a celebrated evangelical preacher but for many a fallen angel who on June 23 turned up in Mexico and reported she had been kidnapped, held for ransom, and then had managed to escape. Was it just a publicity stunt? Had she rendezvoused with a purported lover? No lack of public skepticism here. In January the government confirmed the sentence handed down at a court martial to Colonel

Billy Mitchell. To some he was a hero for his advocacy of naval airpower, to others a troublemaker, insubordinate and intemperate.

Overseas, the world was at peace though the shadows of the Great War still darkened the landscape. Allied debts and German reparation payments remained a troublesome issue. Indeed, Vice-President Charles G. Dawes won the Nobel Peace Prize during the year for his efforts to untangle this explosive issue. Germany was removed from the list of international pariahs when in September it was admitted to the League of Nations. The fact that in November a German in fascist uniform had attempted to kill the president of the Reichstag was disturbing but apparently no cause for alarm. In Italy Benito Mussolini progressively assumed greater control over the nation and at the same time repeatedly survived assassination efforts. Was Mussolini a model ruler or a menace? He had his admirers in America. Leon Trotsky, though he had visited the United States, had few supporters here. When on October 22 he was removed from the political bureau of the Russian Communist Party, few here gave it much thought. Neither did we worry about the disturbances within China or the unrest in India. The dispatch of US marines into Nicaragua seemed little more than a rerun of a familiar script. Short of war, whatever happened overseas was clearly a sideshow for Americans. We had done our share in the Great War some years back. Few Americans were interested in any further involvement. The United States had not joined the League of Nations or become part of the World Court. Americans everywhere were indulging themselves in 1926. Most imagined they could also indulge in the luxury of isolationism.

ODDS AND ENDS IN 1926

- The US Treasury Department estimates the number of millionaires in America to be around 11,000.
- Treasury bonds are issued to yield 3.75 percent.
- First-class postage charge is 2¢ for the first ounce.
- Vincent Vitale loses his life, when on a $5 bet he jumps from the Delaware River Bridge.

- Salary of E. H. Gary, chairman of US Steel, is believed to be $225,000 a year. Bonuses bring it up to $400,000.
- Expenditures for War Department total $355 million. The Navy Department receives $312 million.
- Installment terms usually call for 25 percent down and about one year to pay.
- Queen Marie of Rumania is reportedly offered $25,000 for one day's appearance in the role of the queen in the film version of Tolstoy's *Resurrection.*
- Tickets to hear Commander Byrd tell his story of the first flight to the North Pole cost $1 to $2.50.
- College football coaches' salaries range from $8000 to $15,000 a year.
- Steinway pianos start at $875.
- Mary Pickford and husband Douglas Fairbanks announce plans to build a dream home costing more than a million dollars in San Diego County, California.
- Paul Whiteman and his orchestra sign to do a musical show at a weekly salary of $9500.
- In a divorce granted Kathryn Menjou from film actor Adolphe Menjou, she is awarded the family home plus $100,000.
- The topic of the debate between Columbia and Cambridge Universities: "That This House Rejects the Large Part Played by Advertising in Modern Life." Admission is 75¢.
- Babe Ruth's three-year contract calling for $52,000 a year expires. Responding to rumors that the Babe would next ask for $150,000 a year, Yankee owner Jacob Ruppert replies, "He won't get it."
- The average streetcar fare in American cities is 7.75¢. Bus fare is almost universally 10¢.
- The price of coal in New York City is $14.75 a ton.
- RCA's Radiola 20, radio and loudspeaker costs $150; a seven-tube Neutrodyne Radio is $176 (formerly $315). One of five U.S. families owns a radio set.
- Because of rain and chill, the smallest crowd (38,093) ever, gathers in Yankee Stadium for the final game of the World Series. Scalpers start out trying to sell $5.50 seats for $7.50; then they

quickly reduce them to $3.50; finally in frustration they offer them for $1.

- According to those in the know, more money is bet on the World Series than on any other event in the history of sports. Best estimates are $20 million.
- John D. Rockefeller, Jr., gives $20,000 to assist the proposed flight of Commander Byrd across the North Pole.
- The usual reward for information leading to the arrest of a bank-robber is $2000. Night watchman William Peters receives $2500 reward for foiling a $50,000 bank robbery (February 8).
- British pound sterling rises to $4.86 in February, the highest level since 1914.
- The highest grade oil sells for $3.32 a barrel.
- The winner of a Charleston endurance contest, John Gioia, age twenty-three, dances continuously for twenty-two and a half hours and receives a silver cup and a week's contract at a Broadway theater.
- Kenesaw Mountain Landis, commissioner of baseball, receives $50,000 a year.
- In the eighth race at Tijuana, Mexico (February 3) a year old gelding, Broomflax, finishes second and pays $557.60 for a $2 bet. This is still less than the record paid for place money; that was held by Whiskey Ring at a race at Latonia June 17, 1912. Place money then totaled $644. The price to win: $1885 for $2.
- Children receive $1 for each stray dog they bring in at Bradley Beach, New Jersey.
- In February, Standard Oil Company of Ohio raises its gasoline and kerosene by 1¢, bringing the price of gasoline to 19¢ at a tank wagon and 23¢ at a service station.
- The court martial of William Mitchell, known as the Flying Colonel, costs the War Department $35,000.
- London musicians notify the BBC that they will refuse to play for entertainments relayed by wireless unless they receive extra payments. A Birmingham orchestra requests 5 shillings each for a five-minute broadcast that will be relayed.

• White House maintenance. Cost of Executive offices, staff, and maintenance

1921	$197,000
1923	$349,000
1926	$483,000

• Government Balance Sheet, 1926

Receipts	$3.9 billion
Expenditures	$3.5 billion
Surplus	$377 million
Total gross debt	$19.3 billion

• Average Retail Food Prices, 1926

(per pound, quart, or dozen)

Round steak	37¢
Pork chops	36.8¢
Bacon	47.2¢
Ham	55¢
Lard	19¢
Hens	37¢
Eggs	45¢
Butter	56¢
Milk	14¢
Flour	5.5¢
Cornmeal	5¢
Potatoes	4¢
Sugar	7¢

• Yearly Educational Expenditures per Pupil, 1926

Dallas, Texas	$ 66.80
Rochester, New York	146.63
Birmingham, Alabama	57.83
New York City	114.78
Pittsburgh, Pennsylvania	122.49
Los Angeles, California	129.96
Cambridge, Massachusetts	87.75
Atlanta, Georgia	60.00
Nashville, Tennessee	48.18
Salt Lake City, Utah	73.22
Philadelphia, Pennsylvania	94.38

• Bestselling Books, 1926

Bruce Barton, *The Man Nobody Knows* ($2.50)
A. J. Howard, *Ten Weeks with Chinese Bandits* ($3.00)
Paul de Kruif, *Microbe Hunters* ($3.50)
Edna Ferber, *Show Boat* ($2.00)
A. A. Milne, *Winnie-the-Pooh* ($2.00)

• Stock Prices, 1926	*Low*	*High*
	(in dollars)	
Allied Chemical	106	147
American Express	105⅞	140
American Safety Razor	42	70¾
American Snuff	121¾	165
American Telephone & Telegraph	139⅝	150¾
Baltimore & Ohio RR	83½	109¾
Cuban American Sugar	20¼	30⅜
General Motors	137¼	173½
Hudson Motor Company	40¾	123¼
Loft Candy	6	11¼
Pennsylvania RR	48⅝	57⅛
Pierce Arrow (automobiles)	19	43⅛
Superior Oil	1	5
Union Pacific RR	141½	168⅜
U.S. Steel	124½	130⅛
Woolworth	135¼	222

• Hotel Wagner, New York City, 1926

W. 50th Street & Seventh Avenue
Room for two $3.50 to $4.00
Room with shower
    & bath privileges $4.50 to $5.00
Room with private
    bath & shower $5.00 to $6.00

• Frigidaire Refrigerators, 1926

5 cubic feet	$225
7 cubic feet	$310
9 cubic feet	$395

• Pianos, 1926

Wurlitzer
    Studio upright $295
    Studio grand $625
(Terms as low as $2.50 weekly)

• Car Rentals, Hertz, 1926

	Hourly Rate	*For additional miles over eight, you pay:*
Ford, open	75¢	9¢ per mile
Ford, closed	$1.05	13¢ per mile
Chevrolet, open	$1.05	13¢ per mile
Chevrolet, closed	$1.20	15¢ per mile
Large 6-cylinder gearshift cars	$1.40	17¢ per mile

(All rates include gas, oil, and insurance)

● Chauffeured Limousine, 1926

Straight 8 Packard with uniformed
chauffeur
5 hours or more $4 per hour
4 hours or less $5 per hour
6 hours or less on Sundays $5 per
hour

● Railroad Fares, 1926

Pennsylvania RR (Round trip)

New York City to
   Philadelphia $3
to Atlantic City $3.75
to Washington, D.C. $5
to Danville, Virginia $7
to Pittsburgh $7.50
to Toronto (one way) $17.96
to Boston (by boat) $6

● Fur Coat Sale (skirt length),
  1926

	Original price	Sale price
Russian sable	$13,500	$4500
Hudson Bay sable	$6500	$2500
Broadtail with silver fox trim	$2300	$775
Manchurian black dog	$100	$55
Russian white ermine cape	$2100	$625

● Furniture, 1926

Chest of drawers in mahogany,
with fluted columns plus carved
pineapple tops
  4 drawers $49.50
  5 drawers $58
  6 drawers $66
Four-poster bed in solid mahogany,
with cone-topped posts, head and
foot panels of hazelwood twin
              width $29.50

Coffee table, hand carved solid
walnut, with genuine marble top
              $27.50

● Houses, 1926

Two-story brick, seven rooms, hot
water heat, sun parlor, garage, four
bedrooms, bath. Five minutes to
station.
Larchmont, New York $17,000

English stucco and stone, oak
floors, tiled bath with shower, 14'
× 25' living room with fireplace,
cedar closets, very long plot with
trees.
  Scarsdale, New York $12,600

● Entertainments, 1926

Aida, Metropolitan Opera	$1.50 to $5
John Barrymore in *The Sea Beast*	50¢ to $2
Metropolitan Opera— Wagner Ring Cycle, five matinees	$7 to $25
Beatrice Lillie, Gertrude Lawrence in *Charlot's Review* Balcony	$1 to $2
The Student Prince Orchestra	$3
First Balcony	$1 to $2.50

● New Cars, 1926

Chevrolet roadster	$510
Chevrolet coupé	$645
Chevrolet four-door sedan	$735
Chevrolet landau	$765
Chrysler touring car	$1075
Chrysler roadster	$1145
Cadillacs, from	$2995
Franklin coupé	$2645
Pierce Arrow five-passenger two-door	$2995
Pierce Arrow five-passenger four-door	$3250
Pierce Arrow seven-passenger four-door	$3350
Pierce Arrow limousine	$3450
Essex "6"	$795

● Publications, 1926

Barron's—The National Financial Weekly	$10 per year
The Ladies Home Journal	10¢ per copy or $1.00 per year
The Literary Digest	10¢ per copy
New York Daily News, Sunday	5¢
New York Evening Post	3¢

- Help Wanted, New York City, 1926

(Weekly salary)

Stenographer	$18
Switchboard Operator-typist	$22
Switchboard operator	$20
Assistant bookkeeper	$20 to $25
Legal secretary	$35 to $40
Accountant	$35 to start
Office boy	$12 to $14
Electrical engineer (graduate, no experience)	$33
Chief chemist	$60
Chemical engineer junior	$40
Trader for brokerage house	$1000 to $1300 (per year)
Mechanical engineer	$1560 (per year)
Corporation attorney, experienced	to $7500 (per year)
Lubricating oil salesman	$50 to $75
Teller, experienced	$1800 (per year)
Train conductor	$6.20 (per day)
Baggagemen	$5.20 (per day)
Margin clerk, warehouse	$40
Bank auditor	$2000 to $2600 (per year)

- Men's Miscellany, 1926

Van Heusen collar	50¢
Dutch Master Belvedere cigar	2 for 25¢
Union suits	35¢, $1.39, $1.79
Carter's union suits	$4
Cashmere socks	$1.50
White and blue oxford shirts	$1.85
Nettleton's men's shoes	$12.50
Florsheim shoes	$8.85
Hart, Schaffner & Marx Worsted woolen topcoat	$50

- Women's Miscellany, 1926

Genuine alligator broad strap pumps	$10
Patent leather pumps	$14.75
Knitted blazer	$15
Gray sheer silk stockings	$2.35
Gray suede shoes	$12 to $14
India linen parasol	$3.50

● Travel/Vacations, 1926

Los Angeles to Hawaii, round trip,
    starting at $278.50

Clark's Cruises, around the world
    121 days $1250 to
                      $2900
    62 days in $600 to
    Mediterranean $1700

Steamer travel and rail
One way from New York City to:
    Albuquerque $88.65
    Dallas $68.16
    Houston $63.77
    Los Angeles $107.27
    Phoenix $95.22
    San Francisco $108.90

Fifty-two-day cruise of
Mediterranean
    All expenses,
    New York City $600

West Indies cruise
    Thirty days, plus
    shore excursions $350

Bermuda
    Eight days, all
    expenses $101

New York City to Florida
    Eleven days
    round trip, all
    expenses, tour $132

New York City to Miami
    Boat   from $37.50

New York City to Miami by
steamer,
    outside stateroom
    berth three days $49.72

Miami Biltmore Hotel, Coral
Gables
    Single room   from $8 per
    with bath   day
    Double room   from $16
    with bath   per day

● Used Cars, 1926

'26 Nash four-door sedan	$1495	'26 Chevrolet coach	$550
'25 Dodge sedan	$995	'25 Maxwell coach	$575
'23 Nash sport	$495	'25 Hearns "6" coupé	$1450
'24 Willys-Knight sedan	$845	'25 Peerless five	
'24 Stutz sport touring	$775	passenger, six cylinder	$2000
'25 Studebaker coach	$875	'25 Marmon sedan five	
'19 Cadillac "8" brougham	$475	passenger, 5000 miles	$2200

Capital Punishment

☞ Consumer debt fuels the American economy. Even when it reaches record proportions as it did in 1985 (*18.1 percent* of consumers' disposable income) we encourage still greater indebtedness so that bulging business inventories will not drag us toward a recession. And should we finally exhaust our credit and prove unable to meet obligations, there is the understanding and support of debt counselors and liberalized personal bankruptcy laws. It was not always so. Back in the early nineteenth century the debtor might find himself facing—not counselors—but jailers and debtors' prison. And not much prospect of immediate release, given the obvious difficulty of raising funds while confined. Adding insult to injury, the debtor was responsible for his own support while in jail: food, fuel, and clothing (unlike jailed paupers and criminals who were supplied by authorities). The little guy often wound up in debtors' jails, judging from these figures from New York City in 1809. Of 1152 jailed for debt in that year only 326 owed more than $15. Five hundred were imprisoned for amounts of less than $10! Can you imagine the effect were such laws restored? Who would be left to serve as jailers?

Car Smarts

$11,000 average price
10.1 million sold

$5,400 average price
16.8 million sold

USED

NEW

Aurora '85

☞ There are both new cars and used cars out in the marketplace. But do you know which enjoys higher sales volumes? You've probably guessed right. In 1984 a total of 10.1 million new cars were sold; in the same year Americans bought 16.8 million used cars. A tougher question would be which produced higher dollar sales in that year. If you said new cars you were correct ($97.8 billion to $90.8 billion) except that in every year since 1977 other than 1984 the answer would have been used cars. Of late the spotlight has focused on new car sticker prices (they averaged about $11,000 toward the end of 1984) while most folk would be hard pressed to guess the average price of a used car (about $5400 in 1984. If you knew that there's no need reading further). People with more money buy new cars; those with less, used cars. (Obviously, but here are the figures to prove it. In 1984 the average income of used car buyers was $33,051, while the proud owners of new cars averaged $47,567.) New car, used car, both can't avoid aging. The average age of all cars on the road (reported to be 125.7 million in 1984) continues to creep upward (as it has for the past fifteen years). As prices headed higher people discovered additional reasons to keep their cars. Recently cars had matured to advanced middle age, averaging 7.6 years old (in 1983, 33 percent of the cars on the road were ten years or older). When cars finally lose their drive most are unceremoniously junked. In 1978, a peak year for such departures, more than nine million automobiles stopped dead in their tracks. In an average year somewhat more than seven million cars meet a similar fate. But at least partial reincarnation occurs in the form of auto part transplants.

"Sticker shock" has faded as the public has learned to live with high-priced automobiles. Double digit car price increases are over at least for now. The years of 1980, 1981, and 1982, when prices increased respectively by 10.6 percent, 17.5 percent and 10.1 percent, are now but grim memories. Still that steady advance makes folks downright misty-eyed when they consider what cars once cost. In 1974 the price of a new car averaged $4437. Two years later it was up to $5414, and by 1980 it stood at $7591. The great leap forward occurred in 1981 ($8922) and 1983 saw penetration of the $10,000 barrier. Ironically "sticker shock" could just as well have been applied to used cars. In October 1984, when the price of new cars rose 5.5 percent, that of used cars soared 15.7 percent.

In the market for some pleasant surprises? No one will deny gasoline prices have risen in absolute terms over the past four decades. But introduce the notion of constant dollars (based on dollar value in 1982) and you'll have heads shaking in disbelief when you announce that the price of gasoline was lower in 1982 than it was in 1940! Using 1982 constant dollars the price in 1940 was actually $1.27 per gallon. It dropped to $1.08 in 1950, $1.02 in 1960, and 89¢ in 1970. The gas crunch of 1975 brought the price back up to $1.03, and by 1980 it stood at $1.43. But by 1982 it had retreated to $1.22, a level lower than 1940, and you know what's happened since then. In 1984 American passenger cars logged 1.5 trillion miles (the average driver clocked 8,586 miles) and consumed $79.9 billion of fuel, down by $200 million from the previous year.

Americans were better able to afford their cars in 1984 than in earlier years. They spent $353.9 billion on them and that represented 11.8 percent of their personal income. But consider that in 1983 the figure was 12.7 percent, in 1982 it was 13.8 percent, and in 1980 it was 14.8 percent. So next time you hear someone complaining that car expenses are eating him up alive, be sympathetic but patiently explain how atypical he is. If he remains unconvinced, refer him to this book.

Coaching for Dollars

☞ It's one of the great comeback stories in the world of sports. For years the athletes had grabbed the headlines with their eye-opening salary arrangements. But was it not odd that a coach, annual salary $75,000, was shouting instructions, demanding obedience and performance from a heralded athlete drawing $750,000 annually? If money talks, what was the coach supposed to say or to think in terms of his value to the team?

Well, coaches finally are getting more bucks to go with their bite. Recent managerial contracts indicate how well managers have battled back and are now in contention for the big bucks. In 1985, the Orioles' manager Earl Weaver returned to pilot the Baltimore baseball team for an annual salary of about $500,000. (He had drawn $225,000 before retiring in 1982.) This put him ahead of Billy Martin, whose latest (and short-lived) reincarnation as the New York Yankees' manager earned him a reported $400,000 a year. Managerial comebacks and reunions were obviously much in vogue in major league baseball because, in addition to Weaver and Martin, George Bamburger returned to the Milwaukee Braves who met him with a $300,000 contract.

Outside baseball, other coaches were obviously making the right moves as well. On the gridiron a number of them emerged big winners. Bill Walsh of the San Francisco 49ers led the pack with a contract worth $800,000 to $1 million a year while not far behind was Don Shula of the Miami Dolphins, who was working his way through a four-year $3 million agreement. The old perennial, Tom Landry of the Dallas Cowboys, meanwhile, was making do with $650,000 for keeping that team nearly always in contention.

Apparently coaching five men at a time on a basketball court isn't quite the same as directing gridiron traffic. Matt Guokas of the Philadelphia '76ers signed for a reported $300,000 a year while Stan Albert agreed to put the Chicago Bulls into high gear for a base salary of $350,000. While it is true that hockey salaries are not in the same league as those mentioned here (averaging between $80,000 and $100,000) there's no disputing the fact that professional coaches in general are at long last coming up winners in the great salary sweepstakes.

Coin Costs

☞ The Constitution of the United States grants Congress the power "to coin money [and] regulate the value thereof." In doing so it maintained a tradition long established. Governments have always tried to monopolize the right to produce the coin of the realm. Kings jealously guarded the privilege and made short work of those who dared debase the coins or counterfeit the currency. In this country, Treasury agents have been no less zealous in tracking down those producing or passing bogus bills. The reasons for this great concern are many and mostly obvious. Not the least of which is that it is a source of profit. Printing currency represents a windfall of uncommon magnitude as the costs of production are miniscule compared to the value of the freshly minted cash. Even coins produce healthy profits. Observe the following markups. It takes something less than half a cent to manufacture a penny. With a nickel you're working with about a 100 percent markup given a 2.5¢ production cost. With the other coins the profit picture improves dramatically. A dime represents just 1¢ in product costs, while your quarter involves a cost factor of 3¢. Once you start minting half dollar pieces you're enjoying a 900 percent markup on a 5¢ cost. And there is even more good news. Every producer hopes for repeat business; the mint knows there will be reorders. While the coins don't go out of fashion or become obsolescent they do get lost or are withdrawn from circulation. People for one reason or another put coins aside, save them, or lose track of them. The mint then replenishes the supply with new coins. When it comes to disappearing acts, pennies lead the way by far. Within two years 70 percent of any new batch are no longer circulating. After that pennies fade away at the rate of 7 percent a year. Nickels are less elusive with an annual shrinkage amounting to 7 percent. As coin values increase people tend to become more possessive. Dimes disappear at a 5 percent rate each year and quarters at 4 percent. But if shortages were to develop you could be sure that people quickly would discover an old piggy bank, a bottom drawer, a glass bowl, a cigar box, or some other personal depository, and produce their own source of supply.

Coins and Currency

☞ It takes some stretch of the imagination and a healthy dose of faith to believe in paper currency. What is it after all other than a piece of printed paper? And it is decidedly fragile. Hard currency, that's what Americans, in the early years of the Republic, wanted in their pockets. Actually it was foreign hard currency (Spanish silver dollars, or pieces of eight) that first served as common coin of the country. Before long, however, our government took to minting gold pieces, specifically quarter eagles, half eagles, and eagles (respectively worth $2.50, $5, and $10). They were literally worth their weight in gold, which meant that as they grew old and wore thin they lost some of their original value. Another problem involved fluctuations in the price of gold. When gold prices rose people simply stopped using the coins, preferring to melt them down for their gold content. Meanwhile the govern-

ment introduced additional gold coins, including a dollar and a
twenty-dollar coin and then a three-dollar piece to stand alongside
the original three denominations. For a time private mints were
permitted to get into the act and produce coins of precious metals.
Many were of small denomination and helped ease the shortage
of small change. Not infrequently, however, these coins were discovered to be underweight. Thus discredited, they stopped circulating. Eagles and double eagles ($10 and $20) were not your
everyday coins in the nineteenth century (when they represented
more than a week's wages for most workers). They were used
primarily to satisfy skeptical European creditors who distrusted
American paper currency and to fill bank vaults to comply with
requirements that paper currency be backed by gold and, for a
time, silver. So in fact most gold coins largely retired as everyday
coins as the public grew more comfortable with the idea of paper
currency.

The Great Depression of the 1930s marked the finale of the
golden age of US coins. America abandoned the gold standard,

and gold coin production ceased. Since then the coins have served not as a medium of exchange but as prized items for coin collectors who have seen some of the rarer and more artistically conceived specimens soar in value. In fact, the highest price ever commanded by any coin anywhere, $725,000, went in 1979 for one of the first gold coins known to have been made in the United States. (It was produced in 1787 in New York; only seven are still known to exist.)

President Theodore Roosevelt thought American coins "artistically of atrocious hideousness" and asked his friend, Augustus Saint-Gaudens, the renowned sculptor, to redesign them. His eagle and double eagle, which first appeared in 1907, are considered the most beautiful of all American coins, notable for their deeply sculpted figures. Recently a 1907 St. Gaudens double eagle proof coin brought $260,000 at auction (plus a $26,000 buyer fee). At this same auction, an 1829 half eagle sold for $104,500 and an 1875 three-dollar gold piece for $99,000. "As good as gold" can no longer describe adequately the extraordinary price levels attained by these one-time everyday hard currencies.

Quiz Number 3

1. Average per year pay for first round picks by the National Football League teams in 1985 came to_____per player.
   a) $378,000   b) $225,000   c) $475,000   d) $190,000

2. The total estimated net worth of the *Forbes* 400 richest Americans in 1985 came to_____billion.
   a) 4   b) 25   c) 50   d) 134

3. Over the last fifteen years an investment in the area of_____ would have yielded the highest return.
   a) gold   b) oil   c) US farmland   d) stamps

4. A luxury suite on the *Titanic* (one way) cost_____in 1912.
   a) $1200   b) $850   c) $4350   d) $2100

5. The *Titanic*'s cargo was insured for_____.
   a) $420,000 b) $10 million c) $2.1 million d) $22 million

6. Of the 1985 movies listed below, _____cost the least to produce.
   a) *Perfect*   b) *Pale Rider*   c) *Rambo*   d) *Return to Oz*

7. Dr. Ruth Westheimer reportedly receives a minimum of_____per lecture.
   a) $4,500   b) $10,500   c) $15,000   d) $7,000

8. The average nursing home bill per year is_____.
   a) $15,000   b) $11,500   c) $27,000   d) $21,000

9. An energetic waiter in a busy Manhattan restaurant is said to be able to earn up to_____a day in tips.
   a) $250   b) $125   c) $425   d) $90

10. The highest price ever paid for a champion milk cow at auction was recorded in 1985. The price was $_____.
    a) $150,000   b) $75,000   c) $375,000   d) $1.3 million

☞ *Answers:* 1) a; 2) d; 3) b; 4) c; 5) a; 6) b; 7) d; 8) c; 9) a; 10) d.

Common Scents

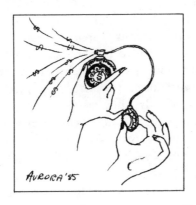

AURORA '85

☞ Generic, copycat, unbranded, knockoff, housebrand. Call it what you will, there's a market for these products. Prescription drugs, cigarettes, paper towels, detergents, the list lengthens. But who would have believed it to include perfumes, whose appeal and glamour seemed so much to depend on image, status, and the hint of extravagance? The brand names still reign (about $3 billion in 1984 sales) but the scent of smell-alikes is in the air. The reasons are obvious. New technology permits close matching to existing products, and fancy brand name prices encourage women to sample imitations. Plus, the numbers favor the imitators whose 75 percent markup dwarfs the 30 percent spread brand producers expect. Both start with a $2 cost for the fragrance; but then the brand manufacturer, whose product will retail for at least $100 an ounce, spends on the average per one-ounce bottle $8 for packaging, $6 for advertising, $9 on beauty advisers' commissions, and substantial overhead costs ($16). The competition spends a total of $1.75 in those same categories. The result is a product that mimics the brand name but retails for about $20 the ounce. Is all this legal? How it's presented is important, but as of now the answer is a qualified "yes." So next time you are drawn irresistibly by a woman's aroma, consider whether she's putting on the real thing or just putting you on.

Concerned Citizens

☞ "Ask not what your country can do for you; ask what you can do for your country." Noble but outdated sentiments? Not to several thousand Americans who each year actually take up the challenge. Their response is to donate money to the government. Yes, you read it correctly; they freely contribute funds to help reduce the national debt. In many cases the dollars come right along with their tax returns. The national debt has yet to be liquidated; still one must nonetheless applaud these public-spirited citizens who in 1982 sent $901,136 off to Washington, and in the following year $911,179. The contributions are, of course, tax deductible, but that should not diminish the significance or nobility of the act.

Contests

☞ Beauty pageant. Egg rolling. Pancake eating. Frog jumping. Spelling bee. All are contests, made in America. It's hard to believe any other country in the world is even close when it comes to conceiving, let alone staging, the kind of contests we do in this country. The following sampler is offered to illustrate the many paths to the ranking of "number one." The behemoths of the gridiron meet annually, not to knock heads, but to clasp hands in the Pro Football Arm Wrestling Competition. The team title, currently held by the San Francisco 49ers, is worth $6000. One moves from behemoths to burros to catch up with the annual Lake Dillon, Colorado, Burro Race. Recreating the old mining frontier days when speed and supplies often meant the difference, contestants race loaded burros some seven miles at elevations of from 9,500 to 12,000 feet. No gold mine at the end of the line here. Just a $600 prize. Fiddlers plentiful then are still making the strings sing today. The best of them may be heard at the annual National Old Time Fiddlers' Contest, competing for a $1400 first prize.

If fast fiddling is not your thing how about fast talking? For this you might want to look in on the annual World Tobacco Auctioneering Championship where style, showmanship, and a quick way with words is worth $10,000. There's only one word sponsors of the Meow Off are looking for. You guessed it. Last year K. C. the cat sounded off smartly and became $50,000 richer with an opportunity for more via a TV acting career. More subdued is Hallmark's National Jigsaw Puzzle Championship; there hundreds compete to put pieces together before anyone else, thereby winning the $7000 top prize. More offbeat is the contest sponsored by Burlington House Draperies. Five thousand dollars to the winner, defined as the entrant having the shabbiest looking window! What else is there to say other than whatever the contest, Americans stand ready to compete.

Cost Overruns

☞ Cost overruns may well be the Achilles heel of our civilization. Consider defense contractors or construction projects or automobile repair bills and what do you find? Final costs well above original estimates. And what of the painter who coats your house, then presents a bill that dwarfs the original "estimate." A lot of unexpected "extras," he explains.

Hollywood often goes haywire in much the same way, hardly a revelation since the movie business has always opted for the lavish over the lean, the massive over the modest. Still a recent book, *Final Cut* by Steven Bach, provides a most revealing movie morality tale. It offers readers the story of how executives at United Artists got sucked into a nearly bottomless pit while they waited for Director Michael Cimino to follow up his highly successful film *The Deer Hunter*, with another blockbuster, *Heaven's Gate*. In-

stead, there came forth a studio buster when huge losses from the movie led to an MGM takeover. The problem was that the movie went $25 million over budget, an eye-opening figure even in free-wheeling Hollywood. Academy Award winner Cimino was intent upon producing a masterpiece and that would take time. Just how much became evident at the end of week one. Already he was five days behind in the shooting, had produced one and a half minutes of usable film, and had spent $900,000. Things did not get better. Often it has been said that there is nothing quite so lavish as a movie production crew out on location. The production of *Heaven's Gate* provided ample evidence of this truth if any was needed. In the end United Artists wrote off $44 million in losses for the film, roundly reviled by most critics and avoided by most filmgoers. (However, the books are not yet closed and auxiliary sales could soften the blow.) Still 1985 saw the release of *Year of the Dragon*, yet another film by Mr. Cimino. One strike and you're not out.

Day's Doings

☞ The production of statistics has become a major growth industry in recent years. Numbers are power; numbers are proof. Numbers are real or so we'd like to believe. Numbers are entertainment, often surprising, at times amazing. If you're looking for those kinds of numbers consider browsing through Tom Parker's *In One Day: The Things Americans Do in a Day*. Parker decided to calculate a day's doings across the United States, probably because no one had ever before thought to produce such figures. Some numbers, the $200,000 worth of roller skates sold, the $12,000 in dental floss, $2.5 million sunk into car washes, or the $40 million ploughed into car repairs, are of interest largely to folks in those respective businesses. Other dollar totals have more character and broader appeal. Our daily bar tab is $64 million. Each day $164 million goes to charities across the nation and $143 million to lotteries. Did you know that prostitutes collect $40 million a day for their services? (Try verifying that total!) In addition, certain other crimes seem to pay. Every twenty-four hours 1000 Americans have their pockets picked and 375 purse snatchings are recorded. The average haul from both these crimes combined works out to $250 per victim. Victims appear elsewhere in Parker's book. Twenty postmen are actually bitten by dogs each day. And to treat them, the US Postal Service spends $3500 a day on their medical needs. Each day we pour $5.5 million into parking meters but are still handed out $16.5 million in parking meter fines. The numbers go on and on. Suffice it to say that here in the United States there is no such thing as a slow day, according to Tom Parker.

Debts, Debts, Debts

☞ "Neither a borrower nor a lender be," Shakespeare has Polonious say, but such words of advice have lost whatever relevance they might once have had. Today they seem downright archaic, even subversive, when we consider that indebtedness is probably the most dynamic element in our economy and certainly the hottest topic around. Headlines speak daily of the mounting Third World debt, US foreign trade deficit, federal budget deficits, corporate indebtedness, and record personal borrowings. Some of the numbers involved seem improbable, almost laughable, and it is in this spirit that the following statistics should be viewed. Aggregate numbers can be annoyingly remote, but try some of these on anyway (knowing that by the time these are read the current figures will be notably higher).

Midway through 1984 the combined indebtedness of the federal and local governments in the United States was $1.8 trillion ($1,800,000,000,000)! Before we become overly judgmental about government irresponsibility, take note that business debt and personal debt each weighed in at $2.1 trillion. This puts the total debt here around $6 trillion. Now one year's interest on this princely sum amounts to about $600 billion and, for whatever relevance it may have, works out to somewhat over $45,000 for each American. (Might each of us at some point be liable for the amount?) If there is any source of comfort it is in our assets. They're worth, or so we are told, $24 trillion, a pretty tidy sum. (Just taking an inventory of these assets represents some fancy figuring.)

Moving from the world of aggregates to individual levels yields numbers more comprehensible but scarcely more comforting. Indebtedness continues to chase right along on the very heels of income. Interest expenses as related to disposable personal income per household have doubled since 1970. Mortgage debt and consumer credit have risen to 18 percent of net worth, while total household debt stands at 83 percent of disposable personal income, a record figure.

When the money starts getting stretched real thin, some people don't get paid, such as bankers. Record levels of home mortgage nonpayment have been reported by the Mortgage Bankers Association. The old record of 5.85 percent of mortgage payments being more than thirty days late has been eclipsed recently by a figure above 6 percent. (The picture doesn't look as bad when you go out sixty days or more; there the figures are just over 2 percent.) Coupled with other bad debts, banks are hurting. When that happens, bank doors begin to close. You've got to go back to the Great Depression to record as many bank failures as we've experienced lately. In the nearly twenty years from 1953 to 1981, 190 banks failed. But then in only three years, 1982 to 1984, that number was exceeded. In 1985 about one hundred failures were recorded, and because the number of "problem" banks has been reckoned at about one thousand, new records are likely to be set. What's the upside here? Misery loves company. When everyone's doing it guilt diminishes significantly. Besides, indebtedness means confidence, otherwise people wouldn't be plunging in, entering that brave new world where such traditional concepts as limited indebtedness are outmoded and downright counterproductive. Feel free to add your own favorite rationalization here. We need all the help we can get.

Depression

☞ Having personal problems? Feeling depressed, angry, anxious? A good friend will probably be willing to hear you out and help. That won't cost you anything except perhaps a request that you return the favor sometime. If, however, you seek out a therapist it will cost you. If it's a top-of-the-line practitioner you're looking for in New York City, expect to pay up to $175 a session. Not for an hour but for a 45 to 50 minute "hour." He or she will schedule you for a precise time months in advance. If you fail to appear—call it resistance, forgetfulness, whatever—you're still out $175. Do such prices accelerate the recovery process? What do you think?

Diaper Change

☞ Changing the baby's diaper will always be one of the more formidable and persistent challenges of child rearing. Few relish

the task. Mothers and fathers both prefer to be unavailable at
such times. As for baby, it cares little who arrives to relieve the
distress so long as someone does. Howling usually helps. Still
there are choices when conditions are not well defined. What to
do about slight staining or mere dampness? Fastidious parents
will not hesitate; too much is at stake, including their self-image
as concerned mothers and fathers and the ever present menace
of diaper rash (palpable proof of their "neglect"). Others may pon-
der the situation not out of distaste for the task but rather its cost.
A change is money. Figure the cover charge at about 17¢ for each
disposable diaper, then consider that the average baby gets in and
out of seven diapers every twenty-four hours. That adds up to
$1.19 a day. Do the rest of the calculations remembering it's no
different on the weekends and that leap year checks in with 366
days. The totals are impressive, and that's just for keeping baby's
bottom dry. Delay toilet training a bit and you've got several years
of diaper disbursements. Improved disposables helped create a
multibillion dollar market (1985 figures are likely to be $3.8 bil-
lion), expected to remain strong as US births maintain their recent
high levels. Meanwhile, the next bonanza will be reaped by the
manufacturer capable of producing the long-awaited and ever elusive leakproof diaper. No price will be too much to pay for such
an advance, one certain to be hailed as only slightly less remarkable
than the completion of junior's toilet training.

Quiz Number 4

1. Basketball coach of Villanova, Rollie Massimino, is
   paid_____a year.
   a) $55,000   b) $82,500   c) $110,000   d) $145,000

2. On Black Tuesday, October 29, 1929, the Dow Jones Bond
   Index closed at 93.13. One year later it stood at_____.
   a) 96.03   b) 31.71   c) 18.22   d) 84.18

3. Recently, _____percent of nursing home bills were paid
   for by the patients themselves. a) 18   b) 50   c) 32   d) 65

4. US life insurance companies invest more heavily in_____
   than in any other area.
   a) corporate bonds b) mortgages c) real estate d) stocks

5. In a recent national survey houses sold for what percentage
   of asking price?
   a) 75 percent b) 98 percent c) 94 percent d) 85 percent

6. In 1984 the average American doctor's net annual income was

   _____.
   a) 86,000   b) $108,000   c) $122,000   d) $157,000

7. In 1960 the annual income considered necessary to
   purchase an average existing single-family house was_____
   a) $12,000   b) $9270   c) $5030   d) $15,650

8. If $200 worth of telephone calls are made from a leased pay
   phone in a New York drugstore, the store owner will
   receive_____from the phone company.
   a) $7.44   b) $16.27   c) $21   d) $32.30

9. Semen sales from a successful bull can approach_____a year.
   a) $25,000   b) $1 million   c) $55,000   d) $100,000

10. In 1985, New York Met pitcher Dwight Gooden received a
    bonus of_____ for winning the Cy Young Award.
    a) $10,000   b) $25,000   c) $35,000   d) $50,000

Doctor Bills

☞ For decades doctors have resisted the idea of fixed fees for their services. Predictably Medicare's current freeze on medical fees is *not* what the doctors ordered. There was a time, however, when medical men accepted fee structures and worked hard to maintain them in particular areas of the country. Here for example is one such effort in Hartford, Connecticut. The year is 1846.

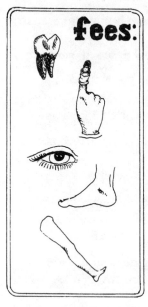

Visiting Fee	$1.00
Consultation (first visit)	$2.00
Traveling fee per mile	50¢
Advice, or extracting teeth at office	50¢ to $1.00
Advice to strangers at office	$1.00
Visits from 11 PM to sunrise	$2.00
Obstetrical fee	$6.00
Dressing wound	50¢ to $1.00
Scarifying eye	$1.00 to $2.00
Cutting gums	50¢ to $1.00
Amputating finger or toe	$5.00 to $10.00
Amputating limb	$20.00 to $50.00
Amputating testis	$20.00
Amputating tonsil	$10.00
Cupping	$1.00 to $2.00
Vaccination	$1.00

For better appreciation of these figures note that shoemakers then made $4 to $5 a week, dressmakers about $2.50 a week, and city printers anywhere from $8 to $12 weekly.

Doctors and Dollars

☞ Why do so many people resent doctors' incomes? After all, they spend at least twelve years at higher education and training, developing unique and precious skills, and then working longer hours than the rest of us (and suffering for it in terms of marital discord, alcoholism, drug addiction, suicide, and so on). Are we envious of their powers over life and death? Do we resent their occasional arrogance or aloofness; or is it our opposition to their profiting from our illnesses? Whatever the reasons, the grounds for resentment, if they ever had any basis, may soon vanish. The golden age of medical practice is fast drawing to a close. Not that the compensation ever was insupportable or much out of line. Today the average physician's income is about $108,400 with predictable variations depending upon region, specialty, and mode of practice. Net average income in New York State is $94,000, in Massachusetts $88,700, in Illinois $105,000. In California it rises to $111,400 and in Florida $134,200. These figures will continue to advance though not by much and probably not beyond general price increases. The doctor surplus is here and it is already leading to an unseemly scramble for patients. Medicare has frozen doctor payments and seems on the verge of imposing fixed fees, long the bugaboo of the profession. Then there are the proprietary hospitals and the health maintenance organizations (HMOs), both of which are bringing doctors onto staff for an annual salary (and therefore with far fewer opportunities for the big money that fee-for-service medicine offers). So you see the sun is setting; the material rewards of medicine are no longer that obvious or inevitable. But then doctors have always insisted it was their love of medicine, their desire to help people and render service, that brought them into the field. Time will tell.

Dollars and Diplomas

☞ Glance up at your college diploma now smartly laminated and hanging prominently in your home or office. No doubt a floodtide of memories will set in—freshman fears, football triumphs, memorable professors, forgettable courses, college buddies, good times, rough times, graduation day. Yet for tens of thousands of Americans their college diplomas usher in no such recollections. What they recall is that the diploma arrived one day in the mail to certify that they had successfully completed courses they never attended from an institution they never saw. These are the graduates of America's diploma mills, the gullible and the greedy who at least were smart enough to realize that without a college degree the dice were loaded against them. But how to get this coveted piece of paper? The answer, it turns out, was simple. Just send for one. Numerous "educational institutions" stand ready to offer instant gratification, either with bogus degrees from reputable colleges or diplomas from paper institutions with such impressive sounding names as National College, South Western University, American Western University, and National College of Arts and Sciences. There will be no teams to cheer for, no college sweatshirts to wear proudly, or campuses to visit; but there will be that piece of paper that might land you the job, get you the raise, or put you in the running for the promotion. And the degree cost but a pittance compared to the astronomical sums often required for four years of undergraduate studies. Besides, you can pick the college degree to fit your budget. Choose from a bachelor's degree for about $800, a master's degree for $1250 (your choice of subject area) and if funds permit, a Ph.D. degree for $2300. (Order two degrees and you might qualify for a substantial discount.) If these figures priced you out, consider South Western University's, which initially offered a bachelor's degree for $575, a master's for $795, and a doctorate for $1050. Still left out? Enroll at North Eastern College of Allied Sciences, the cut-rate college. How about $290 for a BA, $340 for an MA and but $590 for a Ph.D.? And they'll throw in a high school equivalency diploma ($45) and, for twenty dollars, will supply you with a transcript. (None have offered yet to rent caps and gowns.) Established colleges facing declining enrollments are beginning to show some concern over these upstarts. Nonetheless colleges providing cash-and-carry degrees are as elusive as the process of education itself. Flunking them out may be a long and tedious process.

1936

"A total fiasco," "Un-American," "an abominable socialist experiment," "a traitor to his class." These were among the many intemperate attacks directed toward the New Deal and its chief architect, President Franklin D. Roosevelt. A spot reading of headlines throughout the year could convince the reader that Roosevelt's days in the White House were numbered. He had, after all, not brought an end to the Great Depression. Instead he had presided over an extraordinary expansion of the federal government. It now dwarfed the states and was unquestionably the center of power. Had not Hitler, Mussolini, and Stalin traveled along the same path? And much of this government interference, critics declared, had come to little anyway. Recovery would arrive only with the return of the traditional American liberties, only when governmental interference halted.

But much of this was election-year rhetoric. Republicans, long accustomed to seeing "their man" in the White House, imagined Roosevelt to be nothing more than a political aberration. He had won in 1932 because of Hoover's unfortunate association with the depression. This time around the natural majority enjoyed by the Republicans would reassert itself. But Republicans seemed to be losing touch with political realities. The depression was a massive fact in America and Roosevelt and the Democrats understood the toll it was taking on the American people. And they had not stood by idly when the numbers of those in need mounted sharply. True, some of what they did hadn't worked, but then part of it never had a chance to. The Supreme Court threw up numerous constitutional roadblocks to halt New Deal initiatives. The previous year it struck down the NRA (National Recovery Administration), a somewhat heavy-handed effort to stabilize conditions of production and labor across the American economy. Early in 1936 the court gutted the AAA (Agricultural Adjustment Act), one of the more novel and controversial New Deal experiments designed to raise agricultural prices by taking land out of production. And as the year progressed, other New Deal legislation seemed to be in jeopardy. Was the will of the people being unduly frustrated by the Supreme Court? Shouldn't a congressional majority be given the opportunity to try unconventional approaches to unprecedented problems? Conservatives praised the Supreme Court for its fortitude in the face of popular pressure. Roosevelt and his allies in Congress fumed. Was there, they wondered, a way to get around the Supreme Court? Surely a decisive election victory could do no harm.

Actually, the Democratic prospects were quite good for the fall elections. True, the depression still gripped the nation and a severe Western drought brought additional pain, but the administration had a record it could take to the people. It had moved boldly, if not always wisely, to provide emergency relief and keep a very bad situation from becoming positively grim. It had stepped in to put people to work at a time when private industry had little to offer. It had built roads, dams, and schools and had reforested the countryside and decorated public places. It had thrown its support behind labor union organization and collective bargaining, something no other administration ever had dared to do. It convinced millions of Americans that it cared for them. And they responded by turning to the Democratic Party in ever growing numbers.

Still 1936 raised a bumper crop of Roosevelt critics. Not enough money was being spent. The well-to-do were getting off too easily. The unions were being encouraged to act irresponsibly. The deficit was too high, the recovery too slow. Huey Long of Louisiana had gone to his grave the year before, but other critics took up his challenge. Dr. Francis E. Townsend could be heard whooping it up for his old-age pension scheme. Give every person sixty years old $200 a month as long as they promised to spend it. This would spark economic revival, Townsend was sure of it. Father Charles E. Coughlin, a radio preacher with an immense following, found little that pleased him. He took special aim at the government because it paid wages that were below market levels. Roosevelt, he sneered, was no friend of the workers. Then after the Republican National Convention in June, Kansas Governor Alf Landon took to the hustings and added his voice to the opposition forces. His message was beginning to take hold. In fact, one of the more respectable public opinion polls of the day (sponsored by the Literary Digest) had Landon defeating President Roosevelt!

It wasn't even close. Roosevelt overwhelmed the opposition, capturing the popular vote by a lopsided 27.7 million to 16.6 million. Only two states, Maine and Vermont, came through for Landon. Roosevelt was now prepared to move ahead even more forcefully. Stung by his critics, disappointed by the hysterical attacks launched by businessmen whose continued survival he insisted he had helped assure, he seemed ready for bolder, even more controversial initiatives.

The Great Depression and the New Deal were easily the main show but not the only focus of attention. The Pulitzer Prize for reporting in 1936 went to Lauren D. Lyman of the New York *Times* for a story disclosing the intentions of Charles Lindbergh and his family to leave the United States and to settle in England. And just as the year got underway the public learned that in fact Lindbergh had left, citing continuous kidnapping and death threats now directed toward his three-year old son. Bruno Hauptmann, the convicted kidnapper and killer of Lindbergh's first child, continued to proclaim his innocence. But before the year was out he was silenced, executed by the state of New Jersey. Meanwhile federal law enforcement agents were out on the trail making life less than secure for those on the public enemies list. On May 1 agents of the Federal Bureau of Investigation led by Chief J. Edgar Hoover found and seized Alvin Karpis, twenty-six, already declared Public Enemy Number One. G-Men continued to press on. Other hitherto elusive criminals began to feel the heat.

Beyond dispute the sports highlight of the year was the staging of the Berlin Olympics. Germany's Adolf Hitler spared no expense to prepare a majestic setting for the games expected to showcase the superior talents of the Aryan athletes. In fact the Germans did place number one in the unofficial point score but there is no question of who stole the spotlight. The American Jesse Owens, a black man, put on a display that electrified the sporting world. He ran away with the 100-meter and 200-meter dashes, took the broad jump, and went on to collect a total of four gold medals. That combined with a strong American showing in track and field put a damper on German claims to dominance. As it was, just prior to the Games German morale had soared when in a monumental upset German heavyweight Max Schmeling knocked out American boxing hero Joe Louis, another black man. Louis had previously been undefeated. The Brown Bomber recovered quickly from this defeat. Two months later on August 18 he knocked out former champion Jack Sharkey in the third round and in September and October he disposed of two other opponents, both with third round knockouts. Louis was certain he would have his chance at Schmeling again.

In baseball it was the New York Yankees who applied the KO to the competition in the American League, pulling away to victory by a margin of almost twenty games. That earned them a berth in the World Series against their crosstown rivals, the New York Giants. Six games later the Yanks were world champions thanks to the likes of Red Rolfe, Joe DiMaggio, Lou Gehrig, Bill Dickey, and Lefty Gomez.

Traveling to Europe? Some new ways to go became available in 1936. A commercial airship route opened featuring the giant Zeppelin *Hindenburg*. Before the year was out it had completed ten round trip excursions between Germany and the United States (carrying anywhere from twenty-one to seventy-two passengers). In each instance it stayed precisely on schedule and experienced no difficulties. In May the Cunard-White Star passenger liner *Queen Mary* with 2,139 passengers aboard completed its maiden voyage to the United States from England. These were positive developments quite at variance with the steady stream of unsettling news reported from Europe and elsewhere. In Germany Hitler ordered the occupation of the Rhineland, drew closer to Italy's

4444444444

Mussolini, and at home stepped up the campaign against the Jews. In Russia Premier Joseph Stalin proclaimed the new Soviet constitution the "most democratic" of all such documents but insisted there would be no retreat from the dictatorship of the working class or any surrender of authority by the Communist Party. Early in the year the Italians completed the conquest of Ethiopia prompting its emperor, Haile Selassie, to flee. Arriving in Europe he made a dramatic appearance before the Assembly of the League of Nations to plead for assistance. None was forthcoming. Neither was immediate help on the way to the embattled Loyalist forces in Spain who were engaged in a bitter struggle against rebel leader Francisco Franco and his Falangist military forces. In nearby France, interest focused primarily on what might happen now that the nation's first Socialist government, led by Léon Blum, had come to power. Across the channel, England was aghast and the question being asked by all was not who was coming to power but what was happening to the English monarchy. By year's end word spread that King Edward VIII was preparing to renounce the throne so that he could marry the twice divorced Wallis Warfield Simpson, forty-two, of Baltimore. The British Empire would survive this abrupt break with tradition. Other forces were to prove far more destructive.

ODDS AND ENDS IN 1936

- Associated Hospital Service of New York offers subscribers full hospital care coverage (excluding physician charges) for twenty-one days a year, semiprivate accommodations for 3¢ a day.
- First-class mail is 3¢, air mail 6¢.
- Yankee outfielder Ben Chapman holds out for a $12,000 salary. The Detroit Tigers offer $36,000 to Hank Greenberg.
- Each WPA worker costs the government $780 a year.
- The New York state minimum wage law is declared unconstitutional by the US Supreme Court; the law had raised the median wage of women laundry workers from $10.41 per week in 1933 to $13.42 in 1935.

- On March 8, volume on the New York Stock Exchange is 1.4 million shares; on June 2, 786,250 shares.
- The Walter B. Cooke funeral home will provide a dignified funeral for as low as $150.
- It is generally accepted that one can expect to spend two years' income on a house.
- One-third of American incomes are below $1200 per year and another one-third between $1200 and $2000.
- United Airlines plans to spend $1 million to obtain ten Douglass DC-3, 24-passenger planes.
- Actors in the movie *Green Pastures* were paid between $4 and $7.50 a day. Rex Ingram, who played De Lawd, received $1000 a week.
- A 4-grave family plot outside New York City costs $100.
- Paper clips cost 15¢ for 1,000.
- A New York City industrial and vocational school principal earns from $8500 to $10,000 a year.
- Auto insurance rates for New York City come to $90 for the standard $10,000 insurance on bodily injury and $18 for $5000 coverage on property damage.
- The Cleveland Rams are admitted to the National Football League. The franchise cost is $10,000 plus a $25,000 deposit to guarantee all scheduled appearances.
- Irene Dunne, since her successes in *Show Boat* and *Theodora Goes Wild*, is reportedly asking $150,000 a picture.
- Silver prices during the year average 45¢ per ounce.
- Prisoners at the Southern Michigan Prison in Jackson can rent headphones for 25¢ a month and listen to radio stations over three channels.
- An employee of an Ohio bank receives a ten- to thirty-year sentence for his admitted embezzlement of $475,000. The FDIC covered all the bank's losses.
- In May transit employees in San Francisco receive pay raises of 2½¢ an hour.
- Princeton University receives gifts and bequests totaling $304,000. In 1935 the figure had been $569,104.
- The Brooklyn Dodgers pay Casey Stengel $15,500 per year.

- For a six-month period ending October 31, 1936, the Association of American Railroads reports 2,396,162 illegal train travelers and trespassers either were removed from trains, prevented from getting on, or ejected from railroad property. That represents a 31 percent reduction from the same period in 1935.
- Harvard University in December reports that 80 percent of the June graduating class is working.
- In New York City, Bloomingdale's charge cards permit you to purchase up to $30 a month.
- Cost of meals on the Union Pacific Railroad: breakfast 25¢; lunch 30¢; dinner 35¢.
- William Green, president of the American Federation of Labor, declares that America's productive capacity cannot be fully utilized until every family has an annual income of $3600.
- Massachusetts is paying a $10 bounty for shooting wildcats. Seventeen are shot during the year.
- Top New Year's Eve prices at the swankier New York City night spots rise to $15. Cocktails and highballs are sold anywhere from 30¢ to 60¢ each. Champagne is $4 to $10 a bottle.
- Retail sales for the year are 14 percent above 1935 but 24 percent less than 1929.
- Columnist Arthur Brisbane, whose weekly column "This Week" appears in 1,200 newspapers, earns $260,000 a year.
- Convention delegates to New York City spend an average of $100 while there.
- The average apartment rental in New York City is $34 a month.
- Midwestern steelworkers demand $5 a day minimum wage.
- Ticket prices for seats at any of the four Inaugural Balls range from $3.50 to $10.
- A Brooklyn court awards $1500 to a woman whose son died after being clubbed by a policeman.
- The salary of New York City Mayor Fiorello LaGuardia: $40,000 a year.
- Savings and Loan Associations in New York City are paying 2½ percent interest on deposits. The deposits are insured up to $5000.
- The St. Louis Browns baseball team is purchased for $325,000; the price includes its Texas League farm team in San Antonio.

- The American Olympic Committee announces it is $10,000 in the black. The treasurer observes that "every athlete on a major team who actually had to dig into his own pocket to pay his way to Berlin has been reimbursed."
- The average monthly payment by the WPA is $52.50.
- The cost of a New England Christmas Party on the New York Central Railroad including round trip fare, banquet at the famous Wendell House in Pittsfield, Massachusetts, country auto ride, bridge, dancing, entertainers: $4.75.

• College Endowments, 1936

	million
Harvard	$129
Yale	$ 95.8
Columbia	$ 69.5
University of Chicago	$ 65.3
University of Rochester	$ 51.4
Massachusetts Institute of Technology	$ 33
University of Texas	$ 33
Cornell	$ 30

• Christmas Bonuses, 1936

Owens-Illinois Company... 1 week pay
IBM ...... $130,000 given to 3,000 employees
Empire Star Lines $50
Idaho Maryland Mines..... 10 days paid vacation
Johnson & Johnson... 5 percent of 1936 wages
Columbia Pictures ...1 week salary
H. J. Heinz .. 3-year employees get 2 weeks pay (maximum $100)

• Government Salaries 1936

President	$75,000
Vice-President	$15,000
Cabinet members	$15,000
Senate	$10,000
Representatives	$10,000
Chief Justice	$20,500
Associate Justice	$20,000
General	$ 8,000
Admiral	$ 8,000

• Campaign Expenditures, 1936

Republicans	$7.5 million
Democrats	$3.5 million
Communist Party	$157,275
Socialist Party	$20,973

• Retail Food Prices, 1936

(pound, quart, or dozen)

Round steak	34.2¢
Pork chops	33.7¢
Bacon	40.9¢
Ham	48.6¢
Hens	32¢
Eggs	38¢
Butter	40¢
Milk	12¢
Flour	5¢
Corn meal	5¢
Potatoes	3.2¢
Sugar	5.6¢

● Racing Statistics, 1936

Leading Money Winners

	Starts	1	2	3	Amount Won
Granville	11	7	3	0	$110,295
Top Row	2	1	1	0	106,600
Pompom	8	6	2	0	82,260
Bold Venture	3	3	0	0	65,800
Reaping Reward	15	5	2	0	56,965

● New York City Food Prices, 1936

String beans	8¢ per pound
Cabbage	3¢ to 5¢ per pound
Carrots	6¢ per bunch
Celery	10¢ per bunch
Yellow onions	3 pounds for 10¢
White onions	7¢ to 8¢ per pound
Peas	10¢ per pound
Green peppers	3¢ to 4¢ each
Spinach	2 pounds for 13¢
Oranges (medium)	25¢ to 30¢ per dozen
Grapefruit, large	7¢ each
Grapefruit, small	3 for 10¢
Mushrooms	16¢ to 17¢ per pound

● Telephone Rates, 1936

(Every night after 7 P.M. and Sunday all day, for 3 minutes)

New York City to	
Atlanta	$1.45
Boston	$ .60
Chicago	$1.45
Denver	$3.25
Detroit	$1.05
Kansas City	$2.10
Montreal	$ .90
Omaha	$2.10
San Francisco	$4.30
Toronto	$ .85
Philadelphia	$ .35
Pittsburgh	$ .80

● Houses, 1936

Beautiful English home, seven
rooms, three tiled baths, lavatory,
porch, double attached garage.
  Scarsdale, New York $12,500

English garden home, near beach,
five bedrooms, sizable plot
      Rye, New York $7800

2½ acre estate—spacious living
room, paneled library, four master
bedrms, three tiled baths, three
servants rooms, three-car garage,
      Rye, New York $52,500

New colonial, six rooms, large
living room, extra lavatory, not a
development type but individually
planned and constructed
    Great Neck, New York $6950

Nine rooms, two baths, heated
garage, one acre
Stamford, Connecticut $17,000

● Executive Salaries, 1936

(presidents, unless noted)

Alfred Sloan, Jr., General Motors	$374,505
	(bonus included)
William Knudsen, vice-president	$374,475
General Motors	(bonus included)
William Kettering, vice-president,	$249,888
General Motors	(bonus included)
Seton Porter, National Distillers	$100,952
David Sarnoff, RCA	$ 75,840
Martin Condon, American Snuff	$ 54,680
F. L. Maytag, Maytag	$ 45,000
Samuel Bloomingdale,	
Bloomingdale's	$ 75,000
Kenneth Kingsbury, Standard Oil,	
California	$150,075
Walter Teagle, Standard Oil, New	
Jersey	$125,000

● New York City Health
Department Nutritionists' Weekly
Food Budget, 1936

For a family of five (father,
mother, boy 10, girl 6, boy 2)

Milk, grade B,	
14 quarts	$1.54
Milk	
unsweetened,	
evaporated,	
8 cans	.50
Cheese,	
American,	
½ pound	.15
Cheese, pot,	
1½ pounds	.15
Potatoes,	
18 pounds	.27
Tomatoes, fresh,	
3 pounds	.15
tomatoes, #3 can	.12½
Green vegetables,	
10 pounds	.59
Onions, 3 pounds	.10
Dried peas,	
beans,	
2 pounds	.16
Fresh fruit,	
bananas	
(dozen)	.12
other	.10
Bread, whole	
wheat, rye,	
4 loaves	.40
white,	
4 loaves	.32
Oatmeal,	
1 pound	.06

Corn meal,	
1 pound	.04
Butter, tub,	
1 pound	.37
Lard, tub,	
1 pound (or	
1 pint	
vegetable oil)	.16
Sugar and	
sweets,	
3 pounds	.15
Macaroni,	
spaghetti,	
2 pounds	.18
Rice, barley,	
grits, hominy,	
2 pounds	.10
Flour,	
3½ pounds	.17
Eggs, grade B,	
brown,	
1½ dozen	.44
Fish, 2 pounds	.20
Liver, beef, pork,	
or lamb,	
1½ pounds	.38
Chopped meat,	
1½ pounds	.38
Stewing lamb,	
1 pound	.19
Cocoa, ¼ to	
½ can	.04
Coffee, 1 pound	.20
Salt, vinegar	.07
	Total
	$8.05

● New York City Eateries, 1936

Roxy Grill:
Charcoal steak with
vegetable, potatoes,
coffee   75¢
Luncheon of appetizer,
coffee, and dessert   45¢
Full-course dinner   75¢

Paradise Cabaret and Restaurant,
Dinner $1.50—no cover
plus show

Hotel Astor Roof,
Dance to music of Rudy
Vallee, plus dinner $2

Greenwich Village Inn,
Dinner $1.25

Hotel New York,
Dinners   from $1.75

● Entertainments, 1936

Burgess Meredith
in *Winterset*   50¢ to $2
Alfred Lunt and Lynn
Fontanne in   300 seats at
Idiot's Delight $1.10
Ray Bolger in *On Your
Toes* $1.10 to $3.05
Tobacco Road   50¢ to $1.50
Paramount Movie
Theater   25¢ to $1
Astor Movie Theater   55¢ to $2.20
Belmont Park
Horseracing   Men $2.00;
(grandstand)   Women $1.75

● Liquors, 1936

Teacher's scotch $2.69 fifth
Vat 69 scotch $2.69 fifth
Old Schenley $2.29 quart
Fleischmann's gin $1.19 fifth
Martini & Rossi
chianti   93¢ quart
Martini & Rossi
vermouth   93¢ fifth
Cuban rum, ten
years old $1.95 fifth
Four Roses rye $1.64 pint
                      $3.22 quart

● Autos, 1936

Chrysler "6"   from $760
Chrysler Deluxe
"8" $925
Chrysler Airflow
Imperial $1475
Pontiac sedan $615
Oldsmobile "8" $810
Plymouth "6" $510
Cadillac and
Chauffeur $4 per hour
Richfield high
octane
gasoline   18¢ per gallon

● Weekly Salaries, 1936

In Radio:

Executive	$96
Supervisor	$62
Artist	$41
Technician	$35
Office and Clerical	$24

Others

Steno-bookkeeper	$15 to $18
College graduate	$20 to $25
Shipping clerk	$15
Shoe Salesman (ladies)	$25
Dress Buyer	$40

● Miscellaneous, 1936

Philip Morris cigarettes	15¢ per pack
Colgate toothpaste	20¢ large
	35¢ giant
Coca-Cola	six-bottle carton 25¢
Knox straw hats	from $3
London Character shoes	$4.85 to $7.85
Lectro electric shaver	$15
Bell & Howell movie camera	$49.50
Frigidaire, Master Model	$131.50
Coldspot refrigerator, 6 cubic feet	$149 ($5 down)
Gillette razor blades	10 for 49¢

● Travel, 1936

Bermuda cruises from New York City

all expenses	
six days	from $ 74
nine days	from $ 95
thirteen days	from $123

California to Hawaii:

First class	from $125
Cabin class	$ 85

Red Star Line, round trip from New York City:

to England	from $230
to Antwerp	from $238

Train Fare, New York City to:

San Francisco	$85 round trip
Miami	$79.30 round trip
Chicago	$67.05 round trip

Baltimore & Ohio Railroad, New York City to:

Philadelphia	$1.80
Baltimore	$3.75
St. Louis	$21.15

Greyhound bus, New York City to:

Boston	$3.75
Chicago	$14
Los Angeles	$36
Miami	$20
Washington, D.C.	$5.50

Dow Jones

☞ It is to stock averages what Jell-O is to gelatin dessert and Kleenex to tissues. Who amongst us has not heard of the Dow Jones Industrial Averages? Fewer perhaps recognize it as the measure of price trends among thirty selected stocks on the New York Stock Exchange or that it has been signaling price changes since the late nineteenth century (when daily trading volume averaged 250,000 shares compared to today's 125 million plus level of activity). In the early twentieth century the Dow Jones average surveyed the prices of such stalwarts as Studebaker, Central Leather, Remington Typewriter, Utah Copper, and American Beet Sugar as well as American Can, American Telephone & Telegraph, Westinghouse, and U.S. Steel. The list has changed over the years (in 1928 the number of companies included rose to thirty) as American industry evolved and new companies gained maturity and prominence, but the average is still regarded as a bellwether of the economy.

The Dow Jones began at a modest level in 1900 (70.71) and for many years moved within a narrow range. Not until 1909 did it break 100 and some eleven years later at the close of World War I it was still hovering around that mark (95). In the boom years of the 1920s the Dow Jones first began to make its move. In 1928 it rocketed to 300 and in the following year, on August 29 to be precise, it hit 380.33. Then it happened, as many predicted it would. There came the crash, afterward the Great Depression. A previously inflated Dow Jones average went almost entirely limp. On October 29, 1928, it registered 230, recovered a bit in December, and then headed on down as billions upon billions of dollars of stock value simply vanished ($30 billion on October 29 alone!). By September 1931 it was back under 100 at 96.61. It finally bottomed out in May 1932 at 44.74! The 1930s saw some movement but to no great heights. Even the outbreak of World War II barely affected it. (On December 7, 1941, it fell 4 points to 112.52.) New vigor and bounce would not revive it until the 1950s. In November 1954, it finally swept past the old mark of 380 set in 1929 and broke 400. Two years later it reached the 500 level and in February 1959 it registered 600. Lyndon B. Johnson's election as president did wonders for the average, for in January 1965 it reached 900. Speculation mounted as to when it would penetrate beyond the magical, mystical 1000 level. February 9, 1966, saw a brief flirtation (995.15) but Vietnam tremors sent it into a tailspin back to 669 in July 1970. Two years later back it came. And with the reelection of Richard Nixon it went over the top, crashing through the 1000 barrier on November 14, 1972. And today with the average comfortably over 1000, even breaking 1800, analysts speak hopefully of an up-and-coming assault on 2000. Such heights are indeed awe-inspiring. But remember, getting there is more than half the fun and profit.

Easy Rider

☞ Soon enough we'll be celebrating one hundred years of automobile driving in America. No need here to review the impact cars have had on the economy or in changing our lifestyle. It has been, will continue to be, profound. Probably not familiar to most is the part automobiles played in changing spending habits in this country, the consequences of which are still very much with us. Early on producers recognized the automobile's potential as a mass consumption product. Trouble was the price. Relatively few people could afford to lay out the money. (The first Model T of 1909 cost about $900. Prices declined but cars remained costly for the average person.) Henry Ford for one was not concerned. A pioneer in production, he remained a traditionalist about consumption. His cars, he declared proudly, were for the people. All they had to do, if they wanted them, was to save their money. Others had different ideas. Why not encourage immediate possession based upon a partial payment, followed by periodic sums until the full price had been met? Thus was born the installment plan, a revolutionary device that transformed the economy and reversed inbred habits of thrift and established attitudes about consumption. Nothing was out of reach now: no need to defer satisfaction. Now was the time for people to act, thanks to E–Z credit, low down payments and many months to pay. And act they did, first buying cars this way (twenty-seven million were on the road by 1930) and soon a host of other products, which, though not always affordable, had however become necessary. Thus it was in the United States of the 1920s that the American consumer was born. A refrigerator costing $87.50 could be purchased for $5 down and $10 monthly payments. The $28.95 vacuum cleaner required but a $2 down payment plus $4 a month. Seventy percent of all furniture bought, 80 percent of refrigerators, autos, and vacuum cleaners, and 90 percent of pianos, sewing machines, and washing machines were sold on time. The benefits were obvious—immediate gratification, but the price was ongoing personal indebtedness. We've lived with both ever since.

Eat Up

☞ Eating out is "in" these days. Indeed 40¢ of every food dollar spent is said to go to food establishments of one sort or another. Prices at these places have now moderated well below the 11 percent menu inflation in 1979 and the 10 percent rise of 1980. But as always the top restaurants (especially those in New York City that are, or appear to be, French) follow a price path all their own, along which their mostly expense account customers readily follow. Those New Yorkers who remember having a full dinner at Sardi's in 1934 for $1.35, enjoying lobster at the 21 Club in 1939 for $1.75, or consuming a full-course meal at the elegant Lutèce in 1961 for under $20 will lament the passing of those days but still plunk down the $100 per person it takes at some of New York's two dozen top eateries. Why have prices inflated to such gastronomical levels? Expenses can eat you alive. Rent alone at

La Caravelle or Prunelle checks in at $150,000 a year. The latter establishment also chose to spruce up the place with an Art Deco look costing $2 million. For atmosphere La Grenouille turns to nature with floral displays budgeted at about $2000 a week. There is the food, of course, made more costly when knowledgeable patrons request two-inch long carrots ($6 a bunch) or free-range chickens ($9 each), and other imported exotica. And behind the closed doors of the kitchen are the culinary artists with an appetite for paychecks well done. Exceptional chefs may get up to $125,000 a year plus a side order of profit sharing. Less exalted ones can still command $50,000 a year and supervise assistants who are themselves savoring around $39,000 annually. Put all these ingredients together and you have the recipe for restaurant prices that in places are rising faster and higher than the soufflés.

Executive Pay

☞ Interested in running for governor? You're not doing it for the money, but that's no reason not to know current pay scales. They vary considerably. New York is the most generous by far, offering its top officeholder $100,000. Texas is right up there with $90,700 followed by the Garden State (New Jersey), New York's neighbor, at $85,000. California, which quite recently paid its governor a niggardly $49,000 has moved compensation up to a respectable level (85,000). Why, even diminutive Delaware does considerably better ($70,000). On the low end there is Maine at $35,000 and Arkansas parting with the same amount. Does it make any financial sense to run for governor in these two places? The loser surely stands to make out much better financially!

Extras

AURORA '85

☞ So you wanna be in pictures, but a star you're not. Consider starting out as an extra. Don't expect bonanza contracts here. If you want to know what the pay is for those who wander on and off the screen or who serve as anonymous faces in the crowd you need only consult a recent contract negotiated by the Screen Actors Guild. It established minimum daily rates for extras whether in TV or movie productions. If you're part of a passing crowd displaying no notable movements you can expect $87 a day for your work. But get into the action by throwing a ball, running for a cab, or tossing a hand grenade and you're up to a minimum daily wage of $97. Once the camera focuses in on you while you are, for example, hailing a taxi, dealing cards, or playing dead you're now a silent bit extra at $141 daily compensation. Start dancing in a choreographed dance scene and you're entitled to $234. Extras can even make extra money under special circumstances. For riding a motorcycle add $35, but only $12 for being aboard a bicycle. Wearing formal attire nets you $17, while you can figure on $8.50 for each wardrobe change. Don a hairpiece and you can add on $18. An extra $5.50 is yours for each piece of luggage you're asked to carry. And put a little extra into your performance and who knows, you may get discovered.

Quiz Number 5

1. To operate a battleship for a day (fuel, food, crew pay) costs_____.
   a) $56,012   b) $121,040   c) $224,000   d) $1.2 million

2. A Russian sable fur coat can cost up to_____.
   a) $25,000   b) $12,500   c) $55,000   d) $125,000

3. In the magazine field women editors make_____percent of the salaries of male editors.
   a) 78   b) 61   c) 103   d) 92

4. In 1985 the minimum wage for major league baseball players was_____per year.
   a) $82,000   b) $60,000   c) $45,000   d) $70,000

5. The IRS_____impose a penalty on a taxpayer entitled to a refund when the person files late.
   a) can   b) cannot

6. In 1984 the poorest 40 percent of American families received_____percent of the national income.
   a) 28   b) 9.3   c) 15.7   d) 22

7. Top price for a new hot-air balloon is about_____.
   a) $10,000   b) $120,000   c) $92,700   d) $40,000

8. Commission on a trade of 100 shares of a $20 stock will be about_____at a full service brokerage.
   a) $200   b) $60   c) $125   d) $35

9. In the 1920s at the top New York speakeasies, scotch sold for_____a fifth.
   a) $75   b) $15   c) $25   d) $100

10. In 1908 Henry Ford's Model T touring car sold for_____.
    a) $275   b) $1100   c) $575   d) $850

☞ *Answers:* 1) c; 2) d; 3) a; 4) b; 5) a; 6) c; 7) d; 8) d; 9) b; 10) d.

Forbes 400

☞ Every fall for the past few years America's wealthiest individuals and families have discovered just what they were worth. The information didn't come from their accountants or from the IRS. Instead the source was *Forbes* magazine and this information (unearthed by *Forbes*'s own staff of investigators) was then made available to the prying eyes of an envious but respectful public. Envious because wealth stands as the ultimate aspiration in America; respectful because one cannot be anything less than awestruck in the face of such fabulous riches. No shabby millionaires diminish the luster of this list. All 400 are multimillionaires with an individual $150 million net worth as a minimum qualification. All have succeeded far beyond common imaginings, yet what do they have in common?

Our multimillionaires tend to be younger than might be expected, but no brash youths have burst upon the scene. Ten of the group are in their thirties and 52 are in their forties; but well over half are in their fifties and sixties. Few if any can speak convincingly of a rags to riches ascent, but the number of bootstrap operations is impressive. About 165 built their fortunes without inheriting significant amounts of money. Foreign birth was not a disqualification for at least 14 members of this exclusive group. A larger number (181) accepted the less formidable task of holding on to and augmenting sizable inheritances. To a far greater extent than the rest of the population, these folk either recognized the value of a college education or concluded that with their money there was no need to rush onto the labor market. A total of 291 attended college, and 216 were around on graduation day (a far higher percentage than usually prevails among the general college population). To argue that the Ivy League provides the principal conduit to great wealth is to ignore the evidence provided here. True, the two principal feeder schools are Yale (25) and Harvard (12) but among the entire 400 about 56 (or less than 15 percent) were Ivy Leaguers. That money can't buy happiness seems a likely conclusion when 113 of the 400 have been divorced. That a surprisingly large number (79) are unmarried lends itself to any number of interpretations and to an endless flow of hearsay and gossip.

The next generation of great wealth is on its way. These super rich have averaged more than three children per family. If they expect all their kids to qualify for future *Forbes* 400 lists, they'd best continue working to enhance their fortunes and to see to it that their children are similarly inclined. Otherwise they will have to move over or drop out and make room for the next group of brash upstarts ever eager to claim the prerogatives of wealth.

Franchising

☞ Owning your own business, it's the American way. Millions have done it, millions more hope to in spite of the odds, which are formidable. There is, however, a way to improve your prospects. Buy into a franchised operation; link up with a going concern. You're still an owner of sorts but you've reduced some of the risks, eliminated some of the headaches. All you need to get started is investment money and the good fortune to choose a business that is right for you and right for the territory you've been given for the franchise.

While you're mulling over the business for you, let us review the kind of money you'll be called upon to kick in, according to the 1984 Directory of Franchising Organization. If servicing cars was always your secret desire, consider some of the following possibilities. Replacing mufflers can become your thing with a $40,000 investment in a Meineke Discount Muffler franchise. The Midas Touch will set you back quite a bit more, $140,000 and working capital. If transmissions turn you on, $35,000 will get you started either with Lee Myles or AAMCO. It will take quite a bit more, $115,000 to be exact, if you'd prefer painting cars along with the MAACO people.

If the auto field holds no appeal there is still a big world out there. How about becoming a Roto Rooter man (for $5000 and up) or something even more exotic such as (for $25,000) a franchised Port-o-let temporary toilet dealer? If you want to clean up, Merry Maids, a housecleaning service, could be yours for $12,500. Furnishing temporary help has become a permanent business. You're in if you put up $50,000 for a Manpower franchise or advance under the Olsten banner ($25,000 to $30,000). Profit from pets? That's the promise offered by Petland ($20,000 to $35,000) or Docktor Pet ($134,000 to $174,000). Hungry for cash flow? The menu of restaurant franchises is extensive. Fixin' chicken can be done at Church's Fried Chicken ($50,000) and Chicken Delight ($85,000). With burgers there's a choice of Burger Chef ($150,000), Burger King ($200,000), McDonald's ($300,000 and up) and Wendy's ($600,000 and up). If your tastes vary, there is Taco Bell ($150,000), Roy Rogers (about $200,000), and Howard Johnson restaurants ($1 million). For dessert you can savor Baskin-Robbins Ice Cream ($79,000 to $95,000) or Carvel ($75,000).

With all that eating being done, it makes sense to invest in an Elaine Powers Figure Salon ($50,000) or capitalize when folks try sleeping it off at any number of motel chains. Here the figures get a bit steep. Days Inn of America will require $600,000 and Treadway Inn $500,000; but once you move up to Travelodge ($2 million), Howard Johnson (about $4 million), and Sheraton ($5 million to $10 million) you're talking serious dollars. You may then change your mind and apply for a Kampgrounds of America (KOA) franchise ($70,000 and up). So if you want the business, you can be sure there is a franchiser prepared to give it to you.

Free Ride

☞ Tool booths are never welcome sights. They force traffic to slow down, often to a halt. Cars inch forward while drivers grope through pockets for the necessary change. And if it is not the exact change they can anticipate further delays. Because of such inconveniences and the constant expenditure, drivers will go out of their way to skirt tolls. For many, such diversions become an obsession. You can therefore well imagine the reaction when, on rare occasions, toll booths actually are eliminated. Just such a minor miracle occurred in 1985 along the Connecticut Turnpike. A series of 35¢ tolls, long the bane of drivers, were removed. Valuing the time saved, the unfrayed nerves, and the unspent pocket change is beyond easy measure. So too the renewed sense of control over the forces of exaction and restriction—one triumph, albeit small, amidst the more common defeats and disappointments.

Full Page Ads

☞ Full page magazine ads stand a good chance of catching our attention. There are, after all, no other distractions on the page. But such exclusivity costs advertisers dearly. What they pay depends upon how often they advertise (volume discounts) and on the circulation levels of the magazines. For simplicity's sake let us assume a one-time full page, four-color exposure and see what the tab will be (omitting the substantial costs involved in creating and producing the ad itself). One of the more impressive figures comes to us from *Parade* magazine, which will give you a page of their Sunday magazine in exchange for $289,400 (and also provide you with a readership of close to thirty million). That figure is tough to beat but there are other heavyweights in the field, *Reader's Digest* being one of them. Its pages aren't large but still you'll need $104,600 to place your pitch on one of them. *Time* magazine goes down a notch at $114,995 a page. Compared to that *Newsweek*'s $84,390 and *U.S. News and World Report*'s $57,750 are little more than loose change. If you're targeting women, be prepared for a $81,050 charge at *Woman's Day*, $60,800 at *McCall's* and $55,255 at *Redbook*. *Cosmopolitan* can be yours for $40,195. Some fancy figures will also be necessary to reach the sporting crowd. Your product had better be a winner before you hand over

$83,850 to appear in *Sports Illustrated*. If that's too rich for your blood, sign on with *Sport* magazine at $20,800 or *The Sporting News* ($16,728). Kids come cheaper, but it will still cost you. *Seventeen* will ask for $23,475 a page and *Junior Scholastic*, $11,505. The comic books will sell you space, but first you'll ante up a pretty penny for *Marvel Comics* ($17,200) and *DC Comics* ($9850). *Ebony* will place its predominantly black readership at your disposal for $29,990 while the *National Review*, true to its conservative leanings, will only charge you $4000. Other specialty audiences can be yours, from those subscribing to *Dog World* ($2770) to *Firehouse* magazine ($3900) to the loyal devotees of *Weight Watchers* magazine ($8010). Companies pay handsomely to appear before these audiences, but they would pay even more dearly were they unable to reach them.

Government Work

☞ The way we've chosen to arrange things in America, working for the government is supposed to involve some sacrifice. Pay scales are expected to be below those within the private sector. Why accept such second-class citizenship? The work is steady, the benefits good, and in some instances, the experience valuable. Many willingly take high government positions and accept the lackluster salaries. Their long-range plan is to transfer to the private sector, which will pay a premium to former government employees who arrive with an intimate knowledge of the governmental processes. But a recent look at comparative pay scales reveals some unexpected developments. No surprises in the fact that the average salary for a government dentist is $45,440 and for doctors $48,124. Both figures are below community standards. Government lawyers average $38,768, while according to an American Bar Association study in 1983 members of the bar were averaging $52,000. In other categories, however, government workers were holding their own. Librarians at $28,538 fared better than their colleagues outside, while social workers averaging $27,007 easily outdistanced fellow practitioners in the field. Government nurses at $22,742 were over par, while secretaries ($15,826), messengers ($10,352) and guards ($14,495) were also running neck and neck with their counterparts in the private sector. To sacrifice for one's country may no longer be a prerequisite for a government job.

Hired Guns

☞ When it comes to fighting wars, Americans have always preferred volunteers to conscripts. Youthful zeal, patriotic motives, and a man's quest for adventure would, they hoped, result in a sufficient flow of volunteers. True, men came running each time the call went forth, but rarely in numbers sufficient to satisfy military requirements. Clearly additional incentives were necessary, usually in the form of a bounty, normally a combination of land and cash grants. So for example at the start of the American Revolution recruiters offered $10 cash plus one hundred acres of land to anyone enlisting for three years. Soon, however, volunteers became scarce and the Continental Army began offering $20 and by 1779, $200. Part of the increase reflected the intensity of the struggle, part was in response to competing bounty offers. State military forces were in the field along with the Continental Army forcing officials in the various states to outbid federal recruiters. For example, in 1779 Virginia offered $750 in cash plus one hundred acres to those joining its militia forces. Later on, New Jersey advertised its willingness to pay $1000 in cash (though not worth nearly that much given the high levels of wartime inflation).

Bounties brought in the men, often the same men. This occurred when recruits combined enlistment with desertion. Departing cash in hand, they promptly signed up elsewhere, qualifying for yet another bounty. Bounty jumping thus becoming a new form of war profiteering.

Bounties made their last appearance during the Civil War. In July 1861, after Bull Run signaled the end of Union hopes for a speedy victory, recruits were offered $25 in return for nine months of service. The bounty was subsequently raised to $100 and later in 1864 to $300 for new recruits and $400 for veterans who re-enlisted. State and local authorities often added substantially to these figures. (Over the course of the war the federal government paid out over $300 million and the states about $150 million.) But the war dragged on and casualties mounted. In March 1863 conscription became unavoidable. Men were drafted when their names were drawn. Except there was a way out. Paying a commutation fee of $30 was all that was required (at least until the next drawing when your name could come up again). Or you could hire an able-bodied substitute. Paying someone to go in your place (the law required that you appear with him at induction time) was more costly but brought with it a complete draft exemption. The commutation and substitute features of the law made the struggle even more of a rich man's war and poor man's fight. One such well-to-do person, George Templeton Strong of New York, matter of factly noted in his diary that he had hired a substitute, "a big Dutch boy of twenty or thereabouts for the moderate consideration of $1100." He gave the boy his address, even encouraged him to write "if he found himself in a hospital or in trouble." The Dutch boy probably was able bodied, but many a hired substitute wasn't. Furthermore, substitutes were not infrequently experienced operators who pocketed government bounties or private funds for enlistment. They promptly deserted only to repeat the process in some other jurisdiction. A new business emerged featuring substitute brokers who matched those eager to pay with those willing to serve. Many of their transactions did not pass muster, however.

Much the same situation prevailed in the South. One part of the Southern draft law that especially rankled nonslaveholding Southerners was the exemption extended to any slaveholder owning twenty or more slaves. In addition, throughout the Confederacy an active market in substitutes developed. Newspapers carried notices and advertisements for substitutes. By 1863 the market price varied between $1500 and $3000. It rose even higher in places to $4000, $5000, $6000, even $10,000. (Remember as Southern military fortunes fell, so did the value of its currency.) As in the North the system worked poorly and caused considerable resentment. The Civil War taught many a lesson, among them that money couldn't buy fighting men. So in the end bounties and hired substitutes went the way of wooden ships and Confederate currency.

Quiz Number 6

1. Workers in_____enjoy the highest average annual pay in the United States.
   a) Chicago b) Los Angeles c) Anchorage d) Seattle

2. You'll pay the most for three meals and first-class lodging in_____.
   a) Washington, D.C. b) Chicago c) Boston d) Philadelphia

3. The IRS estimates that losses to unreported income and exaggerated deductions now total about_____billion a year.
   a) 25 b) 92 c) 12 d) 134

4. According to the American Medical Association the average medical malpractice award granted by a jury in 1984 was_____.
   a) $338,000 b) $104,000 c) $1.1 million d) $760,000

5. In 1981 the largest recent leap in car prices occurred. Prices rose an average of_____percent. a) 17.5 b) 20.1 c) 13.2 d) 9.8

6. Barney Clark's total hospital bill for the heart implant and subsequent care came to_____.
   a) $110,000 b) $375,000 c) $92,000 d) $250,000

7. In fiscal year 1985 New York State Lottery sales were $1.3 billion. Profits were_____million.
   a) 210 b) 350 c) 615 d) 825

8. Summer box office receipts usually represent about_____percent of total movie revenues for a given year.
   a) 65 b) 25 c) 40 d) 52

9. To be one of the 26,000 individual affiliated members of Lloyd's of London, your minimum net worth must be about_____.
   a) $120,000 b) $200,000 c) $350,000 d) $750,000

10. After ten years' service, baggage handlers and skycaps at airports can expect a top salary of about_____.
    a) $18,200 b) $28,400 c) $15,200 d) $34,600

Incentives

☞ Baseball contracts once were simple documents with clauses as uncomplicated as the country boys who signed them. Not any more. The country boys may still be around chewing on and spitting out their tobacco, but now they've hired a lot of city boys as their representatives, agents, or lawyers who have made the old standard play and pay arrangements obsolete. The new variable is incentive clauses with bonus payments introduced for different performance levels. A look at some 1985 baseball contracts will reveal just how the carrot has been employed to encourage the stick.

Paul Molitar's contract with the Milwaukee Braves begins by rewarding durability. If Molitar shows up at home plate to bat 625 times in a season, add $25,000 to his paycheck. And if he not only arrives but performs well, benefits continue to accumulate. A berth on the All-Star Team will be worth an additional $15,000 to him. Select him as Most Valuable Player and he'll thank all concerned and activate the $50,000 bonus arrangement in his contract. Dwight Gooden of the New York Mets also had his work cut out for him and his incentive awards in place before the 1985 season began. Even had he not won the Cy Young Award and pocketed an extra $50,000 he could still have earned $25,000 for a second place finish and $15,000 for being selected in the third, fourth, or fifth. He was also encouraged to pay attention to balls hit his way by a $15,000 bonus for capturing a Gold Glove Award.

Steve Garvey figures to be a big draw with the Dan Diego Padres, so an attendance clause entered his contract. When the turnstiles at Jack Murphy Stadium spin past 1.9 million, $50,000 extra goes to the former hero of the Los Angeles Dodgers. For every additional 115,000 fans Garvey stood to tack on an additional $50,000. When pitcher Floyd Bannister signed with the Chicago White Sox, his contract bulged with potential goodies. If he pitched his way to the Cy Young Award, $50,000 would be his. A similar award could be claimed were he chosen Most Valuable Player in a League Championship Series or a World Series. As attendance at Comiskey Park rose so would Bannister's compensation. Then there were clauses seemingly more closely related to banking, not baseball. Each year $400,000 of his salary would be deferred, with Bannister receiving 14 percent interest on these funds. And should he face a liquidity crisis, he was free to borrow $200,000 a year from the Chicago ball club. Such rich rewards for sparkling performances now make it perfectly clear why baseball is played on a diamond.

Jock Jack

☞ Are athletes paid too much? That question has been raised regularly over the past few years as salaries escalated to levels hardly commensurate with performing abilities out in the field. Baseball players, for example, in 1985 averaged about $370,000, comfortably above the $11,000 US per capita income figure. But let's introduce some historical perspective. Take the year 1874 if you will and a newspaper story relating the annual salaries of certain members of the Baltimore Orioles baseball team. The catcher, whose name wasn't revealed, nonetheless received $2200. Wood, the second baseman, and Zeitlein, the pitcher, each commanded a $2000 figure, it said, while Cuthbert in left field was worth $1500 and Glenn out in right field $1000. To lend meaning to these figures, the average wage for workers in manufacturing jobs was between $2 and $4 a day, so ballplaying even then yielded above average incomes. Players were not, however, living in the lap of luxury. The article hastened to point out that in the off season Zeitlein was a barber, Wood a machinist, and Cuthbert brought in additional earnings as a butcher.

List Buying

☞ You're listed, indeed many times over. And just about everyone you know is also. You're listed with people much like yourself with regard to income, home ownership, occupation, family size, vacation preferences, religious affiliation, magazine subscriptions, and so on. You're listed because virtually every organization having extensive contacts with the public develops lists of its customers, supporters, and members, then sells them. Yes, your name is being sold all the time and many times over, probably by the approximately 500 list brokers across the country. These people are tracking down useful lists for clients, usually mail order businesses. Direct marketing, as it is called, is a huge, ever growing industry (with over $200 billion in 1984 sales) that depends heavily on targeting potential customers among America's 240 million people.

Prices for lists vary depending on the ease of compilation, competition from similar lists, and their potential value. Thirty-five dollars per thousand names represents the low end. (Prices are

for renting the names for a one-time use only; the names usually
arrive on preprinted mailing labels or envelopes.) You can have
for $35 your choice of the names and addresses of a thousand
drive-in theaters, dude ranches, golf club professionals, pool par-
lors, lobbyists, black elected officials, prisons and correctional facilities, private pilots who own their aircraft, or parents who
purchased photographs of their kids. For more esoteric needs,
expect higher charges. For a thousand dance schools you'll pay
$40, as you will for the names and addresses of swimming pool
contractors or fire chiefs across the country. Lists of magazine
subscribers (another source of revenue for periodicals) will be priced
higher. Subscribers to *Business Week* magazine can be yours at
$65 per thousand (here, as in many other instances, you can obtain
home addresses, often more valuable than places of businesses).
For $60 per thousand you can get a sampling of *Savvy* magazine's
readership, and for $65 those who purchase *Advertising Age*. You
can plug into the world of education with ease. Art professors ($55
per thousand), professors of Portuguese ($34 per), medical school

seniors ($60), and college trustees ($35) are available, as are all other academic-professional specialties. Gamblers can be yours as well. The names of 14,000 people who went to Las Vegas on gambling junkets are available for $1000 per thousand names. Travelers to Europe will be sent to you for $95 per. The consistently higher priced lists nearly always relate to business executives. For $325 per expect the names of 1,000 Coca-Cola franchisees, for $300 the names of new Saudi-Arabian companies, for $350 the names of marketing and advertising executives of sporting goods companies that advertise nationally, and for $110 a list of US executives in the Middle East (terrorists take note).

Want a fix on people's minds and their political and ideological preferences? Forty dollars per will get you a list of opponents to the Equal Rights Amendment while for the same price you can contact folks who contributed to Richard Nixon's 1972 reelection campaign. Another list contains the names of 43,000 businessmen who contributed to conservative causes ($45) while for the same price you can choose from 91,491 "liberals" who oppose budget cuts that hurt the poor. Off on the other side $50 per will buy access to a list of 248,000 national defense advocates.

But you ain't seen nothing yet. Thanks to the ability of computers to match, process, and analyze countless categories from endless series of lists, all sorts of improbable, unexplored permutations are being readied for the coming generation of marketing prodigies. Middle-aged liberals who enjoy hunting? Single parents who are gourmet cooks? Pregnant executives in the advertising field? Pimpled teenagers who've had their licenses suspended for drunk driving? Pinpoint marketing has arrived. We are all targets.

Malpractice

☞ We are currently in the midst of a major public debate on medical malpractice. A crisis is said to exist because of 1) the ever increasing malpractice insurance premiums doctors are facing; and 2) the unprecedented sums courts are awarding plaintiffs, monies that insurance companies are obliged to pay out. Certainly a number of serious issues are involved here, including current levels of medical competence, public expectations of miracle cures, doctor-patient relationships, and the willingness of doctors to enter or remain in certain medical specialties. Nevertheless, the principal focus of public discussion has been on money. Each side has presented its case, made its claims, and drawn its conclusions based on its own monetary calculations. Let's look in on a portion of this debate, noting especially the eagerness of each side to pass the bucks into the discussion.

On the offense are the doctors, hospitals, and the insurance companies, all of whom insist a money crisis is at hand. To make their case they have blitzed the media with dollar figures, eye-catching numbers all. Megabucks, not moderation, is presumably what persuades the public. So we hear of massive malpractice premium increases anywhere from 50 percent to 100 percent (though most are proposed increases, quite different from what is currently in effect and what may in the future be allowed) and are treated to "typical" examples. Enter the Long Island neurosurgeons, who will be paying $101,000 a year for coverage, and the New York City orthopedic surgeons and obstetrician-gynecologists, who will be assessed anywhere from $40,000 to $110,000 a year. One specialty doctor in Florida pays $191,000 a year and two Coral Gables ob-gyns received premium notices for $140,000 each. These figures are startling especially when viewed in the aggregate. Total malpractice premiums paid by doctors and hospitals in 1985 are given at about $2 billion up from $1.4 billion in 1982. And such totals can only keep on climbing because the number of malpractice suits continues to mount. In 1984 there were 40,000 of them, three times the number recorded in 1975. For every one hundred doctors over eighteen suits were being filed, more than double the figure of 1978. And people were collecting: more than $2 billion in 1983 alone. In 1975 the average jury award totaled $94,947, while in 1984 the figure was $338,463. Median awards for birth injuries were $1.4 million (1983/1984) and for surgical cases $456,000. The million-dollar award, once rare, was becoming commonplace. There were but three in 1975, twenty in 1980, forty-nine in 1982, and seventy in 1983. (These are figures from the American Medical Association. Curiously, a New York *Times* editorial put the number of million-dollar settlements at 250 for 1982. In 1985 a spokesman for the St. Paul Fire and Marine Insurance Company, the largest malpractice carrier, was quoted as saying, "We're seeing $1 million verdicts or settlements every week now... Yup. One a week.") But then the dollar figures of settlements are dwarfed by other costs attributed to the malpractice situation. Doctors are, we are informed, now practicing "defensive medicine." In order to protect themselves against future claims they are ordering extra tests, prescribing additional procedures, examining patients more often, an approach that is costing patients a fortune. The AMA puts the figure at 30 percent of the total health care bill (which in 1985 was $387 billion) or an astounding $120 billion a year (but then on other occasions the AMA provided its own estimate of the cost of defensive medicine at $15 billion to $40 billion a year, hardly 30 percent).

The defense has not rested before this onslaught. It has instead countered with its own money figures, calling upon the public to accept them as an accurate measure of the situation. While the medical people employ atypically high figures, the opposition leans heavily on average numbers that they maintain are more representative. Thus the average malpractice premium in New York was not a heart-stopping figure but a more digestible $19,000. And the average doctor spent but 3 percent of his or her gross income for insurance. (Even for the much publicized neurosurgeon, the percentage was a tolerable 5.8.) But why focus on the super specialties practiced in the high rent districts of the nation? Look rather at the Arkansas general practitioner who pays but $1500 a year or at the family doctor from the Midwest whose premium totals $3500 a year. Furthermore, let's put matters into perspective. Total malpractice fees in 1984 were $1.5 billion, but US health expenditures were $355.4 billion. As an expense it was hardly visible (aggregate figures neatly obscure individual cases!). In 1985 premiums rose to $2 billion but so did health expenditures to $387 billion, still a drop in the bucket. (Or put another way, $6 of the average of $1500 spent on the health care for each American goes to pay malpractice premiums.) Nor are lawyers and greedy disappointed patients the culprits. Less than one in ten persons harmed by medical practices ever files a claim. (If a majority of injured persons ever did, then a real crisis would be upon us.) Of those 10 percent only one half gets any money (and nowhere near what the reported settlements indicate). As for the lawyers, they turn away nine of every ten cases presented to them. More attention should be paid to the insurance companies who have managed to sock away a lot of their premium income into unnecessarily large reserve funds (which are then invested and yield handsome returns) leaving a shortage of funds to cover claims, which results in demands for premium hikes. In short there is, opponents assert, no real crisis, only a concocted furor sparked by a relatively few high-visibility doctors who are finding it more difficult to pass on premium increases to the public (and who neglect to mention that their premiums are costs which they deduct as business expenses).

We cannot here dissect the arguments of both sides. But the statistics suggest that when policy battles are joined, figures fly furiously, and bucks, not battalions, are counted upon to determine the outcome.

Meter Feeding

☞ We've been feeding parking meters for years, but they are never satisfied. We've waged war against them relentlessly, yet they have withstood our assaults. We've attacked them, cursed them, jammed them, rammed them, all the while insisting they were little better than rapacious, malfunctioning municipal revenue agents. Our outrage is not without some foundation. When we have nickels they demand dimes; when dimes are plentiful they will only accept quarters. Their timing rarely coincides with ours. This game has been going on for quite some time, in fact ever since meters got their start back in 1935 in Oklahoma City. Since then they have spread out across America until some 7 million of them, according to recent estimates, stand guard duty over what must rank as some of the most sought-after real estate around—parking spaces. Originally intended to encourage circulation and to prevent cars parking indefinitely in one spot, their potential as revenue producers was not ignored. Today many towns and cities look to their meters to produce for the municipal coffers. And they do. Meters in New York City reportedly digest $39 million a year, while in Washington, D.C., the total is $8.8 million and in Los Angeles $7.6 million. Oklahoma City, where it all started, pockets $300,000 annually from its meters. With many modern meters able to retain $40 in coins little wonder that they have become the targets for all manner of thieves from petty criminals to organized rings of official collectors whose regular job it is to empty the meters, albeit not into their own pockets. New York City Mayor Ed Koch made headlines in 1985 when, attending an outdoor function, he observed some meter mayhem firsthand and dispatched his police escort to the rescue, preventing further shortfalls in the municipal treasury. Not all meters are so well protected, however. They will ever remain tempting targets for sabotage, thievery, and assorted mischief.

Middlemen

☞ Producers and consumers alike agree on their dislike, even distrust of middlemen. Down through the years many have tried cutting them out; "direct to you" has been a pitch well known to attract customers. Our farmers have been especially sensitive to the issue of middlemen, especially when they compared retail prices to what they were paid. Here's what the US Department of Agriculture late in 1985 tells us the farmer gets out of each dollar spent on the following foodstuffs. Eggs return 64¢ on the dollar while the figures for beef and chicken are 58¢ and 54¢ respectively. Milk is just about fifty-fifty (52¢ to be precise), while sugar can't be that sweet at 40¢. Back in the pack are white bread (9¢) and lettuce (8¢). So you want to be a middleman when you grow up or even a retailer? Sometime we'll talk about their expenses, their problems.

1946

The war was over but everywhere one saw its consequences. It was time now to come to terms with the new order it had created. The United States continued to test atomic bombs while Joseph Stalin of the Soviet Union denied his country possessed any. The last Germans POWs departed the United States, and German war leaders were put on trial at Nuremburg. Those found guilty were executed; others like Hermann Goering committed suicide. Meanwhile the Japanese accepted a new constitution that renounced the use of war, denied divinity to the emperor, and abolished the armed forces. America, still not over the shock of Pearl Harbor, looked on as a congressional committee attempted to apportion responsibility for that disaster.

Dominating the postwar world would be two great rival powers, the United States and the Soviet Union, whose wartime cooperation gave way to out and out competition, then hostility. The United Nations, newly organized, would provide a world forum but had no formula for peace. Neither did England's Winston Churchill. Speaking in Fulton, Missouri, he warned listeners about Russia's creation of an "Iron Curtain" behind which the Soviet Union planned to extend its domination over Eastern Europe. Western Europe, meanwhile, struggled mightily to restore battered landscapes and shaky economies. Across the Atlantic Americans were encouraged to help out. Sending food parcels overseas would, we were told, relieve some of the hunger and want that was everywhere.

Back home Americans longed for the return of a peacetime economy. The government canceled contracts for war equipment and supplies and struggled earnestly to dismantle the mighty war machine it had assembled. Nowhere could this effort be seen more vividly than over a five-square-mile area in Kingman, Arizona, where some 7,000 warplanes rested side by side, the largest concentration of aircraft ever assembled. All were up for sale at bargain prices. At the same time Americans could hardly wait to launch their own buying spree, to make up for wartime austerities. Retailers, understanding this well, rushed to feature "unlimited" supplies of nylon stockings. Manufacturers promised production and output sufficient to satisfy the pent-up hunger of consumers.

But consumers were still workers first. They had made sacrifices during the war, generally in the form of artificially depressed wages. Now they wanted to catch up. When employers resisted, they went out on strike. Steelworkers, coal miners, railroad workers, meat processors, electrical workers, auto workers, telephone employees—the list of strikers that year goes on. At one point the government threatened to call out troops and draft strikers into the army. Settlements came but were generally regarded as too costly, too inflationary. And what about prices? Everyone knew it was just a matter of time before war-imposed price controls administered by the Office of Price Administration would end. President Truman, bowing to intense pressure, removed most if not all controls before the year was out. To no one's surprise, prices soared. For the first six months of 1946 the inflation rate stayed steady at 3 percent; by year's end there had been a 17 percent leap. Installment buying and indebtedness soared to new highs as Americans were determined to enjoy the blessings and bounty of peace.

During the year historian Arthur M. Schlesinger, Jr., published *The Age of Jackson*, which won the Pulitzer Prize for history. The hero of the book, Andrew Jackson, was described as a larger-than-life figure who dominated the nation's political life and dictated the terms of public debate. By way of contrast, President Harry Truman seemed unable to get a firm grasp on the reins of power. Frustrated by a Congress dominated by Republicans and conservative Democrats and forced to deal with a nation impatient with wartime restraints, Truman's popularity ratings slumped badly as the year progressed. Neither was he helped by the seemingly endless succession of crippling strikes. When Republicans swept both houses of Congress in the fall elections, political pundits confidently predicted that the Democratic domination of national politics was coming to an end.

The world of sports re-emerged from its war-imposed limits as combat veterans returned to the playing fields and spectators turned out in record numbers. The baseball season featured the first playoff in history when the Brooklyn Dodgers and the St. Louis Cardinals tied for the National League pennant. The Cardinals swept the Dodgers to earn the right to go up against the high-flying Boston Red Sox. The Series went the distance with the Cardinals victors in game seven by the score of 4–3. The Cardinal victory provided some consolation since the American Leaguers had devastated the National Leaguers in the All-Star Game 12–0. Named the American League's Most Valuable Player was Boston's Ted Williams. Stan Musial of St. Louis walked off with the honors in the National League. Slugging laurels went to Detroit's Hank Greenberg who, playing his first complete season since 1940, slammed forty-four homeruns. On the mound Bob Feller of the Cleveland Indians erased Rube Waddell's record of long standing. Feller recorded 348 strikeouts for the season.

Out on the gridiron a resurgent Notre Dame, led by Johnny Lujack and ably coached by Frank Leahy, threw down the gauntlet for the powerful Army team, which once again featured the superb backfield duo of Glenn Davis (later named winner of the Heisman Trophy) and Doc Blanchard. The two teams met in New York City before 75,000 fans and played to a scoreless tie. Among the pros the Chicago Bears defeated the New York Giants 24–14 to capture the NFL title. Boxing too enjoyed a resurgence with the staging of the first heavyweight championship bout in four years. Eyebrows were raised and protests mounted when it was announced that ringside seats would be a record price of $100. Excitement centered on the fight between the champion, Joe Louis, and the challenger, Billy Conn, who had in a previous bout stood toe to toe with Louis. This time it was no contest, with Louis the winner by a KO in the eighth round. In what was probably the best match of the year Tony Zale knocked out Rocky Graziano in a middleweight title contest. The year ended with Willie Pep wearing the featherweight crown.

Horseracing saw an exceptional three-year-old run away with the Triple Crown. King Ranch's Assault not only achieved that distinction but also earned record purses for a single season ($424,195). Harness racing enjoyed a banner year with a record $100 million wagered. Golf's big money winner turned out to be Ben Hogan ($42,596) while Lloyd Mangraum won the US Open and Sam Snead captured the British Open. Among the women, Mildred "Babe" Didrikson Zaharias reigned supreme. Out on the tennis courts Jack Kramer proved the dominant force of the National Tennis Championships at Forest Hills while Pauline Betz turned back the competition to win the women's tennis crown. Among the pros Bobby Riggs bested Don Budge for the title.

In the entertainment field Hollywood produced some memorable motion pictures. Walking off with most of the honors at the Academy Award ceremonies was *The Best Years of Our Lives*, directed by William Wyler and starring Fredric March. Olivia de Havilland gained an Oscar as best actress for her performance in *To Each His Own*. Tyrone Power starred in the noteworthy film *The Razor's Edge*, while Gregory Peck and Jane Wyman added considerable luster to *The Yearling*. *Anna and the King of Siam* with Irene Dunne and Rex Harrison offered a unique story in an exotic setting. For comic relief there was Bob Hope and Bing Crosby off on the *Road to Utopia*, while Danny Kaye cavorted through *The Kid from Brooklyn*. Alfred Hitchcock's fans were treated to *Notorious*.

Along Broadway, the season was enlivened by a combination of holdovers and new arrivals. Still around and running well were *The Front Page, Show Boat* (both revivals), *Life with Father, Harvey,* and *Carousel.* The Pulitzer Prize went to a comedy, *State of the Union,* by Russell Crouse and Howard Lindsay; but audiences were prepared to shout the praises of quite a few other major productions, including *Annie Get Your Gun* with Ethel Merman, *Born Yesterday, Call Me Mister, Home of the Brave,* as well as

Finian's Rainbow, The Iceman Cometh, and *Oklahoma!.* Clearly Broadway was back in its stride.

Along the radio waves it was mostly familiar voices and programs long popular. You could tune in the comedy of Fred Allen, Jack Benny, Amos 'n' Andy, Red Skelton, and Fibber McGee and Molly. Walter Winchell headed up the news commentators, Bill Stern the sports news. Soap opera fans could tune in "One Man's Family" and quiz show enthusiasts gathered round the radio for "Information Please." For more serious listening there was a choice between "Lux Radio Theater" and "America's Town Meeting of the Air."

There was no returning to the world as it had been before the War, but many took comfort in the fact that 1946 was far less turbulent than the aftermath of World War I. This time, however, America reigned supreme in the world. It remained to be seen how well it would exercise this leadership.

ODDS AND ENDS IN 1946

• Yale announces tuition for 1947/1948 to be $600 a year.
• A gallon of Breyer's ice cream costs $2.17.
• To mount a Broadway musical costs between $250,000 and $400,000.
• A fourteen-day luxury tour of Mexico including air fare, meals, and hotels costs $499.
• The average employee's hourly rate at the Ford Motor Company is $1.38.
• In February the national debt reaches an all-time high of $279 billion, equivalent to $1832 per person.
• Decca Records borrows $1 million from Chase National Bank at an interest rate of 1¾ percent.
• First class mail costs 3¢ an ounce. Postcards are 1¢.
• Home heating oil averages 8¢ to 9¢ per gallon.
• Trolley and bus operators in Scranton, Pennsylvania, earn 82¢ an hour.
• The average price of a hotel room is $4.23.

- In December silver sells for 86¢ an ounce.
- A bushel of temple oranges (55 pounds) sent from Florida costs $5.50.
- Student benefits under the GI Bill come to $65 per month for single men and $90 per for vets with dependents.
- A Cadillac dealer asserts that a car "sold for $2800 can be resold the next day for $5000."
- Cigarettes by mail are sold by the carton for $1.45 per.
- In New York City, dinner at the Copacabana is $2.75 per person and includes a show featuring Sid Caesar and the Copa Girls.
- New Jersey teachers get a minimum annual wage of $1800.

● Bestselling Books, 1946

Age of Jackson, Arthur M. Schlesinger, Jr.	$5.00
Brideshead Revisited, Evelyn Waugh	$2.50
The Snake Pit, Mary Ward	$2.50
The Columbia Encyclopedia	$19.50
Emily Post's Etiquette	$5.00
Hiroshima, John Hersey	$1.75

● European Relief Parcels, 1946

2 pounds butter, 2 pounds bacon, 30 ounces tongue, 1 pound cream	$ 7.50 to England
35-pound package of food	$12.75 to Greece
6 dozen dried eggs	$3.40 to Europe

● Bowl Games Receipts (Estimated), 1946

Rose Bowl	$450,000
Cotton Bowl	$275,000
Sugar Bowl	$250,000
Orange Bowl	$180,000

● Theater Tickets, 1946

The Iceman Cometh	$1.80 to $5.40
Finian's Rainbow	$1.20 to $6
Carousel	$1.20 to $6
Oklahoma!	$1.20 to $4.80

● War Surplus Airplanes, 1946

B-24 bomber	$13,750
B-17 Flying Fortress	$13,750
B-25 Medium bomber	$ 8250
P-38 Lightning	$ 1250

● Colognes, 1946

Old Spice by Shelton, 4 ounces	$1
Ave Maria by Matchabelli, 2 ounces	$1.50
Intoxication by Dorsay, 4 ounces	$5
Tabu by Dana, 4 ounces	$3.75

● Men, 1946

Boxer shorts	75¢
Broadcloth shirt	$3.98
Remington-Rand electric shaver	$19.50
Marlin razor blades	12 for 25¢
Burberry overcoat	$95.

● Air Fares, 1946

New York City to Detroit via Northwest	$22.55
Newark to Pittsburgh via Pacific Coast Airlines	$14.90
Newark to Milwaukee via Pacific Coast Airlines	$32.85
Newark to Chicago via Pacific Coast Airlines	$32.85
New York City to Minneapolis via Northwest	$45.25
Air travel insurance:	25¢ per $1000

● Concerts & Entertainments, 1946

Rigoletto at the Metropolitan Opera	$1.50 to $7.50
Sonja Henie at Madison Square Garden	from $1.50
Boston Symphony	50¢ to $4
Los Angeles Philharmonic	75¢ to $3.90
New York Philharmonic	$1.10 to $3.90
Philadelphia Orchestra	50¢ to $4
Pittsburgh Symphony	50¢ to $3
Tanglewood	$1 to $5
New York Rangers hockey at Madison Square Garden (general admission)	70¢
Pro basketball— Washington v. New York Knickerbockers	$1.50 to $3

● Selected Stock Prices, 1946 Range

	Low	High
General Motors	$47¾	$80¾
General Electric	$33½	$52
IBM	$195	$250
McGraw-Hill	$23½	$48½
Standard Oil (California)	$12⅛	$50⅝
Texas Gulf Sulphur	$46½	$60¾
American Telephone & Telegraph	$159¾	$200¼
American Tobacco	$73	$99½
International Harvester	$66¼	$102
Average Dow Jones Average for the year:		191.65

● Best & Co. Fur Sale, 1946

	Was	Sale Price
Sheared beaver	$1000	$ 795
Natural summer ermine	$3500	$1995
Black dyed Persian lamb	$ 795	$ 495
Natural otter	$1250	$ 895

● Overseas Calls, 1946

Three-minute call from New York City to:

Iceland	$12
South Africa	$15
Bolivia	$15
Virgin Islands	$ 7.50
Palestine	$13.20
Venezuela	$ 9

● Individual and Family Income, 1946

(percentage of total population)

over $5000 per year	8.9
$3000 to $4999	17.7
$2000 to $2999	30.7
$1000 to $1999	28.7
Under $1000	14

● White Goods, 1946

6 × 7 foot virgin wool blanket	$6.98
17 × 30 inch Fieldcrest face towel	89¢
13 × 13 inch wash cloth	39¢
81 × 108 inch smooth percale sheets	$2.98
21 × 22 inch goose down pillow	$13.50

● Average Interest Rates, 1946

Prime commercial paper 4 to 6 months	.81 percent
Commercial loan rate New York City	1.82 percent
Commercial loan rate, eleven Southern & Western cities	2.85 percent
US Treasury bond	2.19 percent
Municipal bond	1.64 percent

● RCA-Victor Record Albums, 1946

"Panorama," Duke Ellington	$3.31
"Congas," Xavier Cougat	$3.31
"Hot Jazz," Jelly Roll Morton	$4.20
Vaughn Monroe & his Orchestra	$3.94
"Nutcracker Suite," Spike Jones	$2.67

● Average retail prices, 1946

(cents per pound, except milk [quart] and eggs, oranges [dozen])

Wheat flour	6.4¢
Corn meal	6.6¢
Bread, white	9.3¢
Round steak	41¢
Chuck roast	28.7¢
Pork chops	37.3¢
Ham, whole	36¢
Lamb, leg of	40.6¢
Chicken, roasting	47.4¢
Butter	55.9¢
Cheese	38.6¢
Milk, fresh, delivered	15.6¢
Eggs	51¢
Bananas	10.9¢
Oranges	46.7¢
Onions	8.6¢
Cabbage	6.7¢
Potatoes	5¢
Coffee	30.5¢
Sugar	7.1¢

● Blue Cross Rates (New York City), group membership, 1946

Individual	80¢ per month
Husband and wife	$1.60 per month
Family	$2.00 per month

● Houses for sale, 1946

Brick, eight rooms, two and a half baths, finished basement, completely insulated, oil heat.
  Garden City, New York $20,000

New Home, acre, pine-paneled den, four bedrooms, two-car garage, oil heat.
  Darien, Connecticut $32,500

Rental, furnished, waterfront, ten rooms, five baths, large grounds, garage.
New Rochelle, New York
                $5000 per year

Near school, beach, and station, comfortable eight-room house, four bedrooms, two baths, huge playroom.
Westport, Connecticut $32,500

Land
ten miles outside Tampa, Florida
                $30 per acre

Cape Cod Colonial, six rooms, two baths, game room, streamlined kitchen, large plot.
  Scarsdale, New York $24,000

Old Colonial, excellent condition, ten rooms, six bedrooms, three baths, one-half acre, trees, garden, fine old barn for automobile, convenient to town and station.
Greenwich, Connecticut $24,000

● Employment, New York City, 1946

Errand boys	$110 per month	Registered nurse	$200 per month
Telephone operators, starting salary	$28 per week	X-ray technician	$45 to $50 per week
Typist, financial district, thirty-five-hour week	$160 per month	Librarian	$200 per month
		Civil engineer	to $5000 per year
Switchboard operator and typing	$30 per week	Merchandise manager, intimate apparel	$6000 per year
Bank guard	to $40 per week	Science teacher	$2500 per year
Church organist	$40 per month	Advertising art director	$10,000 per year
Social work caseworker	$2100 per year	Insurance claims investigator	$2400 per year
IBM keypuncher	$35 per week		
Medical secretary	$40 per week		
Legal secretary	$55 per week		

Millionaires

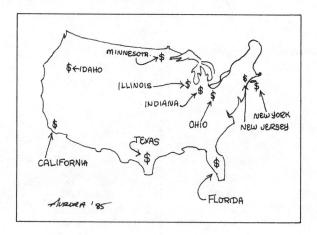

☞ The ranks of America's billionaires are still too thin (of the authenticated billionaires we're limited to fourteen individuals listed in *Forbes* magazine's fourth annual 1985 listing) to attempt an analysis of the breed. When it comes to millionaires, however, they're a dime a dozen and they've been around for some time, at least since the early nineteenth century. (John Jacob Astor was reportedly worth some $25 million, and that before the Civil War.) Recent estimates put the number of millionaires at close to one million. Still they are rare enough to arouse intense curiosity. How much unlike the rest of us are they? Do they fit our imagined images? What do we really know about them?

They are found in all fifty states but like birds of a feather there is some noticeable clustering. (One-half of them live in but ten states.) According to a study prepared several years ago New York, the Empire State, has more than its share. Indeed it holds a substantial lead over California in this category. The only real surprises in a state-by-state millionaire listing are that 1) Texas is only number ten; and 2) that Idaho occupies the number seven position. (Nevada and Wyoming checked in forty-ninth and fiftieth.) Viewed another way and calculating MDs (millionaire densities) you produce such curiosities as sparsely populated Idaho and North Dakota leading the pack. (Idaho in this survey checked in with a record-setting 2,621 millionaires per 100,000 population!)

What we discover about run-of-the-mill millionaires may surprise us ordinary folk. Some do catapult into this category but more typical by far is the process of gradual elevation. Your average millionaire is fifty-seven years old. Ninety percent are married, a notably discouraging statistic for fortune hunters. Lest one discount the value of higher education, note that 95 percent completed at least one year of college and 40 percent hold advanced degrees. That's not to minimize the self-made factor. Very few benefited from substantial inheritances or gifts. In fact over 50 percent received not a red cent from such sources. This bootstrap background may account for their less than lavish taste in lifestyles. One in ten millionaires owns a yacht and one in twenty flies an airplane. Very few (6 percent) have assets that consisted of antiques, coins, stamps, gems, or art. And the most common credit card among the group is not American Express, Diner's Club, Neiman-Marcus, or Saks Fifth Avenue, but Sears! Shall we conclude that millionaires are just plain folks, not unlike the rest of us?

Modest Beginnings

☞ For maximum impact success stories go best with humble origins or meager beginnings. That's because we have so often observed such a sequence of events and remain endlessly absorbed by the possibilities. We all know Benjamin Franklin began as a runaway servant. Few may realize but no one is surprised that President Andrew Johnson was once an illiterate tailor. We are dimly aware that Andrew Carnegie came over as an immigrant from Scotland. But what of more recent examples? Is the old formula still working? Did you know that Marilyn Monroe received $50 for her first nude poses in 1949 or that in 1977 Louise Ciccone (now Madonna) pocketed $10 an hour for similar exposure? Why, even good horseflesh is not always appreciated at first. The legendary John Henry, winner of a record $6.5 million in racing purses, was sold as a two-year-old for $1100. Moreover, who would have predicted the explosive growth and profitability of professional football when in 1962 Ed Sabol (now head of NFL Films) obtained the rights to film the NFL championship game for $2500? Such modest business beginnings abound. Look at what Tom Carvel did with the $15 borrowed from his wife in 1934 so that he could start peddling ice cream. (Carvel rang up $300 million in 1984 sales.) Many of today's billionaires started out with little more. In 1962 Henry Ross Perot put all of $1000 into his startup company, Electronic Data Systems, while David Packard of Hewlett-Packard managed to parlay $595 into a business now doing over $6 billion in annual sales. Billionaire Leslie Wexner (The Limited) borrowed $5000 from an aunt in 1963 on his way to a billion-dollar-plus clothing business, while real estate mogul Harry Helmsley (who controls properties valued at over $5 billion) obviously kept a sharp eye out when he started by working in a real estate office for $12 a week. Enough said. It's time to get a move on.

Money Talks

☞ When conversation turns to money the language is often not far behind. Our coins, our currency, become words, then phrases creating conversation that is colorfully colloquial. It all starts with the penny and heads on up to a million bucks. The lower the denomination the less complimentary the word or phrase generally is, as in "penny ante," "penny pincher" or "red cent." Neither will a "two bit" player be pleased at the characterization, nor everyone patiently accept those contributing their "two cents worth." Few, however, will take offense when a "penny" is offered for their "thoughts," especially if it is a "pretty penny." Saying it with nickels and dimes is usually not a positive sign. What, for example, could be more worthless than a "plugged nickel," less impressive than "nickel and diming" it, or cheaper than "a dime a dozen"? Dollars usually get you more favorable mention especially if you're willing to "put cash on the barrelhead" unless, however, it is "your bottom dollar." But even if your net worth leaves something to be desired someone will bet you "dollars to doughnuts" you still "look like a million bucks." Exactly how to create such an illusion, however, remains for most "the 64 dollar question."

Nickel's Worth

AURORA '85

☞ Don't expect much fanfare but 1986 marks the one-hundred-and-twentieth anniversary of the nickel, probably America's favorite coin. Not that the other coins don't have their supporters and evoke special memories, but the nickel's place in our hearts and in our history is secure. Down through the years nickels were able to buy what young folks prized most. The soft drink for a nickel, the hot dog, the 5¢ candy bar, chewing gum, and the comic book, amusement park rides, and earlier still, entry to the nickelodeon. A nickel's worth of an item might just amount to something. And when they grew up the nickel's usefulness remained— for telephone calls, popular magazines, a newspaper, a schooner of beer, a shoeshine, or any number of items in the five-and-ten-cents store. With the passage of years the nickel steadily lost ground and value, and nickel items all but disappeared. Five cents could still buy pencils, gum, nails, needles, peanuts, balloons, and an occasional novelty, but none of the old-time favorites. Today the list is painfully small—some small candies, two for 5¢ Tootsie Rolls. Even the parking meters are rapidly changing over to dimes and quarters. The nickel will remain, its usefulness for change undiminished (especially with untaxed $1.95 and $2.95 items) but the not so small pleasures once associated with it are now but dim memories, drifting off, then vanishing much like the smoke from a 5¢ cigar.

Quiz Number 7

1. Of the officials listed below, the highest salary belongs to the_____.
   a) vice-president   b) speaker of the House   c) chief justice of the United States   d) US senator

2. The average professor's salary is highest at_____.
   a) Stanford   b) Tulane   c) Syracuse   d) Baylor

3. Those individuals with famous names but unknown faces are paid_____by American Express to do the commercial.
   a) $10,000 to $15,000   b) $25,000   c) nothing
   d) $5000 to $10,000

4. Stunt drivers performing risky maneuvers can make about_____a day.
   a) $1500 to $2000 b) $8000 to $9000 c) $5000 d) $750

5. In 1983 the Senate voted to limit additional incomes of members to_____a year.
   a) $50,000   b) $12,500   c) $20,940   d) $35,000

6. Studies of the IRS indicate that every dollar spent on auditing yields_____in income.
   a) $5   b) $16   c) $10   d) $32

7. The median black family income is about_____percent of median white family income. a) 82   b) 55   c) 72   d) 88

8. In the late 1920s the net profit per year of Al Capone's crime syndicate was estimated to be_____million.
   a) 62   b) 14   c) 120   d) 6

9. The amount of money gambled legally in 1984 amounted to_____billion. a) 243   b) 26   c) 71   d) 147

10. Esso's 1972 name change to Exxon in the end cost_____.
    a) $18 million b) $200 million c) $70 million d) $35 million

Nobel Prizes

☞ These are good times, maybe even the best of times for Nobel Prize winners. The prestige remains enormous and the cash payments higher that ever. Thanks to Alfred Nobel and the considerable sum of money he set aside for this purpose (between $8 million and $9 million) there are handsome awards awaiting those cited for their outstanding efforts in science, medicine, literature, economics, and for the advancement of world peace. The reward in 1985 was a record $225,000 in each category, strong evidence that Nobel's funds have been well administered of late. The payments, you see, do vary each year depending upon how effectively funds have been invested. Win during a period of lackluster money management and no matter how glorious your achievements you're obliged to settle for a lesser cash award. Catch a good year and you will be well rewarded for your accomplishments.

In the early years of the prizes (first awarded in 1901) payments hovered around the $40,000 mark. In 1930 when Sinclair Lewis gained the prize for literature payment had risen to $46,350. It soon slipped back to about $40,000 with the coming of the Great Depression. Prizes were not awarded in the early years of World War II and when they resumed in 1943 the money award took another drop. When the International Red Cross received the Peace Prize in 1944 payment amounted to $29,059 and in the following year when former US Secretary of State Cordell Hull won the peace prize it had inched back up to over $32,000. The 1950s saw no dramatic gains; it was not until 1963 that the $50,000 level was surpassed. Reflecting the inflationary decade of the 1970s the Nobel cash awards grew substantially in those years. In 1970 Russian writer Aleksandr Solzhenitsyn was awarded $78,000 but six years later the American novelist Saul Bellow took home $160,000. Mother Theresa might have done better but she had the misfortune of winning the Peace Prize in 1979 when the award dipped to $145,000. By 1983 it had risen to $190,000, the sum that Poland's Lech Walesa received as the Peace Prize. Just two years later the award leaped to a record $225,000.

Take note of one additional factor. A rapid survey of past recipients reveals that the selection committee, especially in the sciences and medicine, tends to choose more than one winner. This means splitting the pie. The peace, and literature, and economics prizes ordinarily have gone to a single individual and so winner takes all. Those still uncertain of their life's work should take note.

Off the Beaten Track

☞ The age of discovery has long since passed. No longer can we venture to lands unknown or stumble upon portions of the globe yet unexplored. Still we can read about those who first ventured into Africa, penetrated the jungles of South America, or drove headlong to the North Pole and sense their excitement, thrill to their discoveries. Or we can retrace their steps and in so doing summon up a sense of adventure notwithstanding luxurious accommodations and well organized tour guides. Having your cake and eating it too seems to be the object of a new series of tours designed to break away from the humdrum hauls over to Paris, London, Spain, Puerto Rico, or Hong Kong. An outfit called Society Expeditions of Seattle, Washington, typifies this new approach to adventure for the affluent. Here's a sampling of what they offer.

If you're inclined toward crusty old Europe you can do it but in a way that recalls an older era of romance and adventure. For ten days you'll travel aboard the Orient Express in deluxe period accommodations (circa 1920s and 1930s) as this fabled train makes its way from Paris to Istanbul. (Cost of train trip alone is $4990.) If Europe seems old hat here's a place off the beaten track: the Yemen Arab Republic. For sixteen days you can observe such points of interest as Sana'a, Mamakha and Ta'izz most economically ($2990 for the Yemen trip itself). If you're still into ancient exotic remote kingdoms you can next try Tibet for seven days out of a total twenty-day expedition into the region for $3990 (excluding airfare). If you prefer sea level to the Himalayas consider the twenty-four-day cruise into the South Pacific, visiting such places as Fiji, the Solomon Islands, Guadalcanal, and New Guinea. Price for the cruise itself starts at $5690, but if you prefer the best suite aboard ship, plan on $13,650. If the balmy breezes of the South Pacific are not for you, there's a way to cool off by heading to the North Pole on an eleven-day tour beginning in Edmonton, Alberta, and concluding with a flight to the North Pole. There's room only for twelve on this one (at $7950 each). If you're not among the lucky twelve you might consider the thirty-five-day cruise circumnavigating Antarctica. That one starts at $8990 and moves up steeply to $27,950 for the best accommodations. If cruises are not your speed how about heading off for an around the world in thirty days flight aboard a private jet limited to just thirty passengers? Sound good? If you've got an extra $29,450 a reservation can be yours. Finally there's a chance for true adventure as an extraterrestrial being. Come 1992 and coinciding with the five-hundredth anniversary of the first voyage of Columbus, Society Expeditions is cooking up a flight into space, the last frontier, aboard a specially designed twenty-passenger space ship with lift-off from a US government launch site. Plans are for some eight to twelve hours in flight, enough time to complete anywhere from five to eight orbits of the earth. Weightlessness and panoramic views are guaranteed. Be the first on your block to sign up (cost: $50,000).

If you're a stick-in-the-mud you'll not be moved by any of this. But to those of sufficient wealth and persistent wanderlust, the gateway to adventure beckons.

Paying Professions

☞ Most everyone would agree, whether or not they even know the actual figures, that doctors, lawyers, accountants, all of them, charge too much and are overpaid. But there isn't much heard about college professors. Of course it can't cost all that much to live in an ivory tower.

Before having a look, a note of caution. Evaluating academic salaries based upon full professors is akin to judging Broadway's pay scales by looking at the names on the marquee. What's missing is the supporting cast. And at colleges and universities, that crew often outnumbers the full professors by a wide margin. These people, often instructors, adjuncts, or assistant professors, are the migrant laborers of academe. A course here, a course there, before moving on to teach the next crop of undergraduates. The pay is by piecework and is paltry. Each course pays $1200, $1500, maybe even $2000. Teach a few courses and it still doesn't add up.

The full professor, on the other hand, will teach the same number of courses, perhaps four a year, and get paid $40,000, $50,000, sometimes $60,000, depending on the institution and seniority level. And then, there is still most of June, July, and August to reflect upon the deeper meaning of things. One of those things could well be the declining real incomes of academics. All full professors are not equal, even in institutions that feature uniform salary schedules. Outside pressures and priorities do make themselves felt within the university.

What the real world deems important ends up being more richly rewarded by university administrators. So while full professors of foreign languages average $41,530 a year, engineering professors receive $47,341, according to a recent study of public institutions. Education professors, presently attracting little attention, are taking home relatively little income—$38,431. Computer science, on the other hand, quite in vogue now, must pay professors $48,000 to pass on their knowledge to eager students (while probably permitting unusual moonlighting privileges as well). The picture for fine arts professors is not bright at $37,818, while professors of business are sitting atop the pay curve at $47,424.

But all will have to go some to unseat the current champions, law professors. They are presently averaging $58,077, quite handsome for college faculties. But otherwise it's a sacrifice, considering that top law firms are swooping down on selected first-year law students with offers in the $50,000 range. Still, the classroom is to be preferred to the courtroom. There, professors, right or wrong, nearly always win.

Pennies

☞ It's not a good sign. Remember, as kids if we saw a penny lying on the ground, in an instant we'd be diving for it, considering it our lucky day. Well that's hardly true any longer. A walk down most streets will reveal many a penny resting undisturbed on the sidewalk or along the curb, coins that are in full view of passersby. Folks just don't consider it worthwhile to stop and pick them up. Can you imagine such willful neglect? There are even people who, if they happen to drop a penny or two, will not bother to retrieve them. Thus the penny has come upon hard times, a victim of inflation, and suffering perhaps from the infirmities of old age. The Lincoln penny is after all the oldest American coin currently in circulation. Issued in 1909, it was also the first coin to bear the likeness of an American President. (Others followed suit including the Washington quarter in 1932, the Jefferson nickel in 1938, the Roosevelt dime in 1946, the Kennedy half dollar in 1964, and the Eisenhower dollar in 1971.) With few exceptions (such as those pennies minted in the early 1930s) substantial quantities of each coin were produced making unlikely any present or future increase in value. But it would not be wise to predict the disappearance of the penny. So long as consumers continue to swallow the bait of 79¢ items or two for 99¢ deals, the penny will have a useful role to perform.

Perennial Pinball

☞ It was not long ago that we were bemoaning the loss of the younger generation to video games. These computerized sirens were, it was said, sucking the kids dry, making off with their lunch money, even forcing them into lives of petty crime in order to appease their habit. The once proud and lucrative pinball machine, where it even managed to survive, was shoved into a corner, remnant of a more primitive era. Revenue gains from video games were breathtaking. In 1979 a billion dollars flowed in while two years later the figure rocketed to $4.8 billion. In 1982 your average pinball machine brought in $40 a week at the same time that a video game was contributing $70. But then, quite suddenly, you could hear yourself talk at a video arcade. The kids began staying away; 1983 revenues were back down to $2 billion. The players were becoming bored; they were leaving the computer patterns; the games were becoming predictable. Meanwhile revenues from pinball games clocked in at $2 billion, just about where they had always been. Was the tortoise about to overtake the hare once again?

Peripatetic Pranks

☞ The service society is here to stay. Indeed our continued economic growth depends on it. So we can only applaud the appearance of yet another vital service—live entertainment messages. Ever since Western Union bowed out of singing telegrams the stage was set for new entrants and more elaborate presentations. For about $40 you can still have your message delivered melodiously, but far more entertaining are the costumed messengers who rely less on singing and more on the element of elaborate ruse and surprise. If you're interested in a little fun at the expense of a lady friend, consider dispatching a nerd. An unmistakably wimpy character will turn up, ask to see her, then insist that they have been matched by a computer dating service. Her protests notwithstanding he will insist upon a date. For your $65 to $75 he will maintain the charade anywhere from five to seven minutes. A somewhat more intimidating figure is also available at the same price. The Arabian Knight will, at your behest, descend upon an unsuspecting woman and demand that she return to his harem. Insisting upon his prerogatives he may just convince bystanders of the righteousness of his cause. Women can exact revenge by having a "policeman" venture forth to arrest the "victim" or by dispatching a 250-pound opera singer to work her wiles on an unsuspecting fellow. The cast of characters is endless and the talent generally good enough to play their parts with conviction. Aspiring actors and actresses usually work this entertainment circuit, hoping perhaps to be discovered during one of their command performances.

Quiz Number 8

1. In 1983 the average annual compensation for members of the board of directors of major corporations was_____.
   a) $16,990   b) $24,950   c) $31,600   d) $37,000

2. In 1947_____received the highest salary in baseball.
   a) Ted Williams   b) Joe DiMaggio   c) Bob Feller
   d) Hank Greenberg

3. The Washington Monument was completed in 1884 at a cost of_____.
   a) $125,000 b) $1.2 million c) $6.5 million d) $15 million.

4. In New York City and Los Angeles, a well established movie director can get_____a day for filming a commercial.
   a) $5000 to $6000   b) $20,000 to $25,000   c) $10,000 to $12,000   d) $30,000 to $40,000

5. Independent truckers in a good year will average_____.
   a) $42,000   b) $57,000   c) $15,000   d) $26,000

6. In 1983 the average veterinarian's pretax income was _____. a) $76,000 b) $29,000 c) $41,000 d) $57,000

7. ABC agreed to pay_____million to cover the Winter Olympics in Calgary in 1988.
   a) 200   b) 622   c) 275   d) 309

8. One could buy Texas Longhorns in the 1860s for $3 to $4 a head and then sell them up north for about_____each.
   a) $12   b) $40   c) $95   d) $18

9. In 1982 when the hourly wage in the US garment industry averaged $5.20, it averaged_____in South Korea.
   a) $1   b) 35¢   c) $1.75   d) $3.25

10. Salaries in the NBA 1984/85 averaged_____.
    a) $325,000   b) $175,000   c) $401,000   d) $210,000

Plane Facts

☞ What does it take to keep an airplane in the air? Profits! And in the new free-wheeling deregulated environment, airlines are having to work harder for them. Here's what they're up against. They need people filling seats, though not as many as you might think. In 1984 the major airlines operated at only 59.3 percent capacity. Looking over the past few years the break-even point was generally between 53 percent and 54 percent. So even if you see a lot of empties on your next trip it is probably still a money-making flight for the carrier. Airlines also have to keep fuel costs down. Every one-cent drop in the price of fuel translates into a $100 million saving in operating costs for a major airline. On this front the news is good, after being very bad. Back in 1978 jet fuel was an affordable 38¢ a gallon but three years later it skyrocketed to $1.02. Fortunately it's down again, averaging about 83¢ toward the end of 1984. What also has to remain reasonable, at least from the airline's viewpoint, are labor costs which represent about 35 percent of operating costs. In 1983, for example, the average industry-wide compensation per employee was $42,505, a level easily beyond that of any other American business. Travel agents also take a sizable chunk of the airline pie. In 1984, for example, the airlines paid out $2.5 billion to travel agents, a figure representing 7.5 percent of total operating costs. Still, without those agents the airlines would be obliged to establish an elaborate and costly ticket distribution network of their own. Now that you understand the basic economic framework of the airline industry, you might wish to consider acquiring a few planes and flying off into the "friendly skies" for fun and profit.

Play Ball!

☞ Here's how some recalled the experience. Mike admitted it was the "most fun I've ever had with my clothes on," and George conceded, "I got goose bumps." Dan still gets "choked up just thinking about it," while to Maury it had to be "emotionally one of the highlights of anybody's life." To Mickey it was simply "a dream come true." Okay. You figure it out. The birth of a child? The marriage of a daughter? Clever guesses both but incorrect. The sweet recollections above all were memories of a week out in the Florida sun playing baseball. And these were not green rookies excited over their major league prospects but middle-aged men, breadwinners all, reliving their childhoods.

Baseball marketing has reached yet another level of sophistication. Why wait for the season to begin? What's the point of letting spring training facilities go unused a good part of the year? Take advantage of the little boy in every American male. Allow him to live out moments once confined to his most private thoughts, his most vivid fantasies. Had he only had the chance he could have hit major league pitching, could have fielded with the best of them, could have been a star. Well, that chance is now, a bit late perhaps but still that glimmer of what might have been surely will come through.

The New York Mets call it Dream Week. Other major league ball clubs bill it as Fantasy Week. The Los Angeles Dodgers market it as the Ultimate Adult Baseball Camp. All operate in much the same way. A week away at spring training facilities following a routine similar to that expected of major leaguers—workouts, instruction, practice session, intra-squad games, locker room chatter. And all this taking place under the supervision of major league players. Real live Mets will mingle with and compete against the "pay for play" types. The Dodgers typically have gone one step better. They've loaded up on Hall of Famers including Ernie Banks, Al Kaline, Bob Feller, Juan Marichal, Sandy Koufax, Harmon Killebrew, and Duke Snider. No run-of-the-mill ball players for this baseball camp.

In addition to the games come the gimmicks. With the Mets it includes a uniform, a video of Dream Week highlights, and a set of major league baseball cards complete with photo and individualized stats. Some of the glowing comments with which we began now become understandable. Could heaven on earth offer more? Before heading South mention of the bill should bring many down to earth. Compared to the Dodgers the Mets charge a modest $2795 complete for eight days and seven nights of cavorting. The Ultimate Baseball Camp is priced accordingly—$4995. Play Ball!

Pockets of Plenty

☞ Looking for pockets of plenty in this country? You won't find them all over the map or even where you might have expected. According to a recent study of family income within the nation's 37,000 Zip Code districts, most of the top twenty were concentrated in just a few locations. Not one was in oil-rich Alaska, surprisingly none in Texas, forget Florida, cross off the South, and practically the entire interior of the nation. So just where are these aggregations of the affluent? Predictably California was represented by Beverly Hills (number three) and one other community, and there was Glencoe, Illinois, and a section each of Boston and St. Louis. After that, however, it was almost all New York City. The New York metropolitan region accounted for nearly fifteen of the top twenty areas, bedroom communities all with families living mostly off the wealth generated in and around New York City. Long Island represented the mother lode with six of the top twenty including number one, Great Neck (median family income $74,552), and number two, Roslyn ($70,330). There was also Saddle River, New Jersey; Darien, Connecticut; and Chappaqua, New York, in well-to-do Westchester County; along with other suburban areas on the periphery of the great metropolis. So it seems that despite talk of the Sun Belt, Oil Wealth, Silicon Valley, New Wealth, Trickle Down, and all that, your run-of-the-mill affluents still are mostly where they've always been.

Presidential Provisions

☞ He starts at $200,000 a year and gets $50,000 for expenses and $100,000 for travel plus a free house. Compared to chief corporate executives this compensation package is not all that generous. But that's only the beginning of what it costs to maintain the president of the United States. When you're finished calculating entertainment, security, staff, travel, communications, and the like, tens upon tens of millions have been expended. It was not always that way. Parsimony, not pomp, was the style Americans once thought best suited the White House and its occupants. The original presidential salary of $25,000 did not seem all that stingy (not until 1873 was it raised to $50,000) but from that sum the president was supposed to cover all expenses associated with the office. It couldn't be done. Washington added $5000 of his money, Jefferson nearly $20,000, and Monroe claimed he ended up $30,000 in the red. When presidents tried to use available public monies for expenses, as John Adams did with a horse and carriage and John Quincy Adams with a pool table, they were sharply rebuked by Congress. Washington, Jefferson, Madison, Monroe, Jackson—all of them came upon hard times after leaving office. Except for extraordinary grants by Congress, no provision was made for maintaining ex-presidents. Out of office meant off the public payroll. It is not until we get to Harry Truman that Congress in its generosity agreed to provide ex-presidents with a pension (at first amounting to $69,630 a year). Presidents once came cheap; they no longer do.

AURORA '85

1956

All things considered, the news on the homefront wasn't all that bad. The FBI got their man, six of them in fact, who in 1950 had pulled off the Brinks Robbery, the largest in US history. The assistant US surgeon general announced that no child who had received the three Salk polio shots died of polio during the year. Three weddings made the headlines. One was a quiet affair held out in Independence, Missouri, where Margaret Truman, only child of the former President, married Clifton Daniel, assistant editor of the New York *Times*. The other generated considerably more interest because the couple, playwright Arthur Miller and movie queen Marilyn Monroe, were both public personalities. The third marriage was an event of the first magnitude, reported on by about 1,500 newspeople. Joined in matrimony were film star and all-American beauty Grace Kelly and her Prince, Rainier III of Monaco. The 20,000 inhabitants of that principality couldn't have been happier. An heir would mean continued exemption for them from French taxes and military duty. After separate civil and religious ceremonies, the couple sailed off on the prince's yacht for a Mediterranean honeymoon. Then some four months later came the much awaited official announcement. Princess Grace was expecting.

It could have been far worse when on July 25 the Italian luxury liner *Andrea Doria* collided in the fog with the Swedish vessel *Stockholm* some forty-five miles off Nantucket Island. Aboard the Italian vessel were 1,709 passengers. A goodly number of the lifeboats were put out of commission by the collision. Fortunately, rescue calls were picked up by other ships, most notably the *Ile de France*. In the end all but ninety-five of the passengers were rescued.

President Eisenhower also had a close call during the summer when he underwent surgery for ileitis. This, combined with his heart attack the previous year, raised doubts about his ability to seek and win a second term. Once doctors declared him fit, however, Ike dismissed talk of retirement and along with Vice-President Richard Nixon soundly defeated his Democratic challenger, Adlai Stevenson.

That atomic energy could be applied to peaceful uses moved closer to reality when the Atomic Energy Commission approved the construction of two private atomic plants designed to produce electricity. A reminder of the atom's more lethal uses came from the skies when the United States dropped a hydrogen bomb over the Pacific in the first airborne test of this most devastating of weapons. That civilization would as a result hang in the balance one day no longer seemed so far-fetched a proposition. On the other hand, civilization did withstand the TV appearance of rock singer Elvis Presley on the "Ed Sullivan Show." This idol of millions of teenagers had already sent shock waves through an older generation with his raucous music and pelvic gyrations. Did his appearance on a family show such as Ed Sullivan's indicate the coming domestication of Elvis? A less heralded event was the arrival in the United States of Canadian teen-aged singer Paul Anka. He had come to record a song, his own, "Diana."

The United States was at peace but it was troubled. Two years earlier the Supreme Court, in a landmark decision, declared the legally established segregated public schools, long the rule in the South and some of the border states, to be unconstitutional. Rather than comply with the ruling the South chose a campaign of resistance. In Congress Southern members presented a manifesto calling upon both the Senate and the House of Representatives to employ all means possible to reverse the Supreme Court's decision. States passed laws enabling authorities to channel funds away from public schools and to sell off public facilities rather than see them desegregated. In many places black children attempting to attend all-white schools were turned away as National Guardsmen stood by to avert violence. Autherine Lucy managed to enroll at the previously all-white University of Alabama, but soon afterward was expelled. Authorities in Montgomery took legal action early in the year against the Reverend Martin Luther King, Jr., and other blacks for leading an illegal boycott against the city's bus lines. Violence simmered just below the surface and at times burst forth. Again in Birmingham, whites beat up prominent pop singer Nat "King" Cole during a performance there. A divided nation deferred decisive action. The American Bar Association voted in favor of complying with the Supreme Court decision against segregation. The vote tally, 118–101, made it clear just how hard that would be.

Across the world the Cold War continued unchecked and while each side floated disarmament schemes of one sort or another, few held out much hope of progress. But many in the West hailed the harsh words of condemnation coming forth from the Soviet Union and directed against a former leader of that nation, the late Joseph Stalin. The "cult of personality" exemplified by Stalin was roundly denounced. Russia would, they said, be better served by a new form of collective leadership. But before the year was out the Russian leadership would have cause to regret its denunciations of Stalin. Eager to test the dimensions of this new and more liberalized posture, citizens of Poland and then Hungary rose up in opposition to their existing Russian-dominated governments. Rallying behind Wladyslaw Gomulka in Poland and Imre Nagy in Hungary, they pressed for a relaxation of controls and the removal of Russian troops. Matters grew tense in Poland but the explosion never came because both the Russians and the new Polish leadership backed off. Adjustments in the system would be forthcoming. Hungary could not be so contained. Open revolt brought Russian troops and tanks into Budapest. The expected bloodbath followed; Russian power prevailed. As thousands of Hungarian "freedom fighters" fled the country they were received as heroes in the West and admitted into the United States.

There was no shortage of other hotspots. In Kenya British officials pressed on in their efforts against Mau Mau terrorism. While both Tunisia and Morocco gained their independence, the French had no intention of allowing the same for Algeria. That brought Algerians into open revolt against French rule with the outcome very much in doubt. Reports from Cuba indicated that an armed revolt was underway against the government of Fulgencio Batista. Although the rebels had staged an unsuccessful attack against an army post in Matanzas, they appeared capable of mounting a serious threat to the Batista regime. Not far off in Nicaragua assassins ended the life of the country's strongman, Anastasio Somoza. Just who would now take hold of the reins of power was not at all clear. In the Middle East the ongoing skirmishing between Israel and its Arab neighbors erupted into something far more destructive. The decision by Egypt's President Gamal Abdel Nasser to nationalize the Suez Canal was but the first step in a series of subsequent moves that ended with the seizure of the canal by the invading forces of Israel, France, and Great Britain. Ultimately a United Nations peace force moved in to enforce a truce but no one was naïve enough to believe much of substance had been resolved in the region.

Back home one career was just beginning, that of the first gorilla to be born in captivity, while another somewhat more illustrious one came to an end. Rocky Marciano, thirty-one, the undefeated heavyweight champion, decided to call it quits in April after forty-nine professional bouts, leaving a vacancy at the top, one filled later in the year by Floyd Patterson when he knocked out Archie Moore in Chicago. Among other notable pugilists during the year were Sugar Ray Robinson, Ezzard Charles, Gene Fullmer, Kid Gavilan, and Willie Pep. The horseracing champion of the year was three-year-old Needles, who nearly captured the Triple Crown, losing out (to Fabíus) in the Preakness. Still Needles held the lead in total winnings among the year's fastest thoroughbreds. The track was fast and clear for the New York Yankees, who ran off with the American League pennant leaving Cleveland far behind. Over in the National League the Brooklyn Dodgers just squeezed by Milwaukee and Cincinnati to capture the title there. But once the two pennant winners gave battle in the World Series no one was surprised when it went down to the wire. It was not until game seven that Yankee power dashed Dodger hopes as New York blasted four home runs, sending Don Newcombe and a host of other Brooklyn pitchers from the field. The Yankees were now world champions but fans were still buzzing about events in game five. On October 8 at Yankee Stadium Yankee pitcher Don Larsen accomplished what no other moundsman pitching in a World Series ever did. He pitched a no-hitter and a perfect game. The Dodgers never even got a man to first base! Dodgers fans found some solace in the fact that their heroes bounced back in the following game when Clem Labine blanked the New Yorkers. Other individual stars illuminated the baseball diamond during the season. Mickey Mantle of the New York Yankees led the American League in batting with a handsome .353 and was named Most Valuable Player. Brooklyn's pitching ace Don Newcombe, despite his failure in game seven of the Series, posted a sparkling 27–7 record and was selected as Most Valuable Player in the National League. Milwaukee's Henry Aaron took batting honors in the Senior Circuit posting a .328 season average. Frank Robinson of the Cincinnati Redlegs was named Rookie of the year, an honor he shared with Luis Aparicio of the Chicago White Sox, named the American Leagues best rookie player.

Over on the gridiron there were all-Americans aplenty. Many of the standouts were certain to be heard from again once they entered the professional ranks. This lineup included Ron Kramer, Joe Walton, Johnny Majors, Alex Karras, Jim Parker, John Brodie, Jim Brown, Jack Pardee, and Paul Hornung. Hornung, the much heralded quarterback of Notre Dame, was named winner of the Heisman Trophy. Conference champions included Iowa in the Big Ten, Oregon State in the Pacific Coast Conference, Tennessee in the Southeast Conference, and Texas A & M in the Southwest. Over in the professional ranks it was the New York Giants all the way; they overwhelmed the Chicago Bears, winners of the Western Conference, 47–7 in the championship game.

It was an Olympic year and so off to Melbourne, Australia, went the athletes of sixty-nine nations (five countries withdrew in protest against the Russian invasion of Hungary). The Russians put in a consistently strong effort and came away as the unofficial winner with a point total of 722 compared to the 593 compiled by American athletes. As always Americans dominated the track and field events. Bobby Morrow ran away at 100 and 200 meters, Tom Courtney placed number one at 800 meters, Charles Dumas took the high jump, Bob Richards the pole vault, Parry O'Brien the shotput, Al Oerter the discus, and Harold Connolly the hammer toss. Australia, thanks to a strong showing in swimming, finished third, followed by Germany and Hungary in the overall point totals. Just prior to the opening of the Olympics the sporting world was saddened by the death of an athlete who was truly Olympian in her talents and achievements. Mildred "Babe" Didrikson Zaharias succumbed to cancer in Galveston, Texas. Back at the 1932 Los Angeles Olympics Didrikson had won two gold medals and had gone on from there to demonstrate why many consider her the most skilled and versatile female athlete of the modern era. After displaying a remarkable proficiency in basketball, baseball, tennis, and track and field, she decided to concentrate on golf. Here she swept the field, winning eighty-two titles along the way. The world may never again encounter an athlete so far beyond ordinary capacities.

For those who found their entertainment away from the fields of sport there was much from which to choose. Among the best sellers of the year, two concerned Massachusetts politicians. *The Last Hurrah* by Edwin O'Connor was a work of fiction but *Profiles in Courage,* written by John F. Kennedy, junior senator from the Bay State, surveyed crucial events and heroic decisions from the American past. The devotees of reincarnation could find support in *The Search for Bridey Murphy* by Morey Bernstein, while backdoor gossipers had much to savor in the steamy *Peyton Place* by Grace Metalious. More established authors had their entries for the year including Alec Waugh's *Island in the Sun,* Nelson Algren's *Walk on the Wild Side,* and Graham Greene's *The Quiet American.*

Off at the movies many of America's most popular actresses had featured roles. The lately departed Grace Kelly could be seen in *High Society* while high society Texas-style was the background for *Giant,* starring Elizabeth Taylor. Audrey Hepburn was caught amidst the turbulence of the Napoleonic Era in *War and Peace,* while closer to home the screen sizzled from performances by

Carroll Baker in *Baby Doll* and Marilyn Monroe in *Bus Stop*. Everyone enjoyed traveling *Around the World in Eighty Days* and watching Yul Brynner at his majestic best in *The King and I*. This time around Gary Cooper was reluctant to fight, playing a pacifist in *Friendly Persuasion*, while Kirk Douglas was off playing artist Vincent Van Gogh in *Lust for Life* and Charlton Heston assumed the mantle of Moses in *The Ten Commandments*. When the dust had settled and the Academy Awards announced, Brynner had his while honors for the best picture went to *Around the World...*" The lovely Ingrid Bergman won Best Actress for her performance in *Anastasia*.

Over on Broadway a number of plays from the previous year were still packing them in, including *The Diary of Anne Frank, No Time for Sergeants, The Matchmaker, Fanny, Damn Yankees,* and *Inherit the Wind*. Add these to the theatrical happenings of 1956 and Broadway truly dazzled. On March 15 Rex Harrison and Julie Andrews opened in a musical based on a work of George Bernard Shaw. Critics raved and predicted *My Fair Lady* would take its place among the classics of Broadway musical comedy. The following week the multitalented, buoyant Sammy Davis, Jr., opened in *Mr. Wonderful* and just kept going. Musicals continued to dominate the scene with the opening later in the year of *The Most Happy Fella, Li'l Abner,* and *Bells Are Ringing*. For hectic comedy, *Auntie Mame* was your best bet but for a more serious evening it would be *Separate Tables*. Great drama but little joy would be found in Eugene O'Neill's *Long Day's Journey into Night*.

As usual television offered mostly light entertainment. Masters of the genre included Perry Como, Dinah Shore, Jackie Gleason, Phil Silvers, Lucille Ball, and such favorite programs as the "Ed Sullivan Show," "Your Hit Parade," and "The $64,000 Question." Edward R. Murrow's news commentary often hit the mark while no one could fault Lassie for all-around abilities. Among the more memorable shows of the year were "Peter Pan," "The Caine Mutiny Court Martial," and Rod Serling's "Patterns," an original play for television. The spread of color sets was now beginning to accelerate. By the end of the year 250,000 were in American homes. Prices were coming down; the future seemed bright indeed.

ODDS AND ENDS IN 1956

• Figures released during the year reveal that median income last year for men was $3400 and for women $1100.

• The IRS announces it has received an envelope containing $2500 in hundred dollar bills. The sender was listed as I. O. Thismuch of Chicago. The money is placed in the "conscience fund," which the IRS says receives contributions of about $10,000 a year.

• Brunswick introduces its automatic pinsetter for bowling alleys. It will sell for $7700.

• The Federal Reserve raises the rediscount rate from 2½ percent to 3 percent during the year. Prime commercial borrowers are paying an interest rate of 3¾ percent.

• Radio revenues rise .9 percent from the previous year, but television income shows a spurt of 25.6 percent.

• Less than one of three cars is bought with cash.

• Attendance at the New York Metropolitan Opera averages 93.6 percent of capacity, the highest level in its history.

• Hofstra College announces new minimum pay scales for its faculty: Professors $8000; associate professors $7000; assistant professors $5000; instructors $4000.

• The Detroit Tigers bring a record price for a major league baseball team, $5.5 million. The record had previously been held by the St. Louis Cardinals, who were bought in 1953 by August Busch for $4.5 million.

• Television is used extensively by both presidential candidates for the first time in a campaign. Estimates are that $6 million was spent both for TV and radio time.

• Independent theater owners vote Kim Novak and Susan Hayward the top money attractions for actresses, while William Holden and Frank Sinatra make the best showing among actors.

• Yogi Berra receives the third highest salary ever paid by the New York Yankees ($58,000). Ranking ahead of New York's star catcher are Joe DiMaggio ($100,000) and Babe Ruth ($80,000).

• Estimates of net spendable income after tax and social security deductions for average production worker with no dependents are $67.79; with three dependents $75.20 (based on gross income of $82.42 weekly).

• Consumer debt reaches all-time high, $36 billion or 12.2 percent of disposable income. Stores report bad debt losses of less than half a percent. Federated Department Stores reports that about 60 percent of purchases are on credit.

• Offset printing costs $7.25 for one thousand 8½ × 11 inch sheets. Five thousand sheets cost $22.25.

• New York City spends $3.84 a day per person each to maintain its prison population.

• For an eight-week summer camp experience for your child, prices range from $350 to $525.

● Hardcover Book Prices, 1956

MacKinley Kantor, *Andersonville*	$5
Herman Wouk, *Marjorie Morningstar*	$4.95
John O'Hara, *Ten North Frederick*	$3.95
Anne Lindbergh, *Gift from the Sea*	$2.75
John F. Kennedy, *Profiles in Courage*	$3.50
Norman Mailer, *Deer Park*	$4
Jim Bishop, *The Day Lincoln Was Shot*	$3.75
Edwin O'Conner, *The Last Hurrah*	$4

● Television List Prices, 1956

Black and white:	
GE Portable	$99.95
Hoffman 14-inch Portable	$139.95
17-inch Admiral	$149
17-inch RCA	$199
21-inch Admiral	$269
20-inch Philco	$325
20-inch Motorola	$325
21-inch GE	$329
21-inch Zenith	$395
24-inch Magnavox	$449
Color:	
RCA	$795 to $895

● New York City Restaurant Tabs, 1956

Le Chanteclair:	
Lunch	$2.50 to $2.75
Dinner	$3.85 to $5.50
Dubonnet:	
Seven-course Dinner	$2.50
with prime Ribs of Beef	$3.50
with prime Sirloin Steak	$3.95
Gramercy Park Hotel:	
Complete family dinner	from $3
McGinnis's	
Seven-course dinner and cocktail	$3.95

● Governors' Salaries, 1956

New York	$50,000
New Jersey	$30,000
California	$25,000
Massachusetts	$20,000
Connecticut	$15,000
Alabama	$12,000
Idaho	$10,000
North Dakota	$9000

● Broadway Theater Ticket Prices,
  1956

My Fair Lady	$2.30 to $8.05
Damn Yankees	$1.15 to $7.50
Fanny	$2.50 to $7.50
Pajama Game	$1.75 to $6.90
The Matchmaker	$2.50 to $5.75
Inherit the Wind	$1.75 to $5.75

● Indianapolis 500 Finishers, 1956

	Purse
1. Pat Flaherty	$93,819
2. Sam Hanks	$32,919
3. Don Freeland	$20,419
4. Johnnie Parsons	$15,769
5. Dick Rathmann	$10,744

● Ike's Proposed Budget, 1957/
  1958

Total Spending	$ 72 billion
Military Spending	$ 38 billion
Air Force	$ 19 billion
Navy	$ 10 billion
Army	$ 9 billion
Foreign Aid	$ 4.2 billion
Atomic Energy Commission	$ 2 billion
Interest on Debt	$ 7 billion
Total Indebtedness	$271 billion

● Houses, 1956

Center hall, seven sunny rooms,
three family bedrooms, three
baths, maid's room, large screened
porch, attached garage.
  Scarsdale, New York $34,750

Colonial ranch, new, three
bedrooms, two baths, complete
electric kitchen.
  Greenwich, Connecticut $31,600

Cape Cod, four bedrooms,
den, two baths.
  Darien, Connecticut $32,600

Large eight-room colonial, four
bedrooms, one and a half baths,
thirty-foot living room, large
modern kitchen, screened terrace,
finished attic, hardwood floors in
basement.
  Westport, Connecticut $29,500

Levittown Home,
  Levittown, Long Island   From
                             $9190
  $690 cash $71 per month

● Liquor Prices, 1956

Calvert Reserve Whiskey	$4.50 per fifth
Romanoff Vodka	$3.98 per fifth
Fleischmann's Whiskey	$4.25 per fifth
Schenley	$4.50 per fifth
	$5.55 per quart

● Positions Available, 1956

	Weekly Salary		Weekly Salary
Female:		Wall Street mail clerk	$2600 per year
Gal Friday	$65	Cafeteria manager	$150 per week
Executive secretary	$85 to $100	Chef, A-1 restaurant	$175 per week
Switchboard operator	$60	Accountant with degree	$8500 to $9000 per year
TV Show secretary	$70		
Airline Reservation trainee	up to $280 per month	Insurance claim examiner	$5500 per year
IBM keypunch operator	$65 to $70	Sales trainee	$4420 per year
Clerk	$56		
Law secretary	$90	Assistant bookkeeper	$60 to $65 per week
Receptionist, attractive, no skills	$50	Copywriter	$100 per week
Editorial assistant	$70	Boys	$40 to $50 per week
Countergirl	$57 (plus meals)	Cabinetmaker	$2.50 per hour
File clerk	$40 to $55	Bank clerk trainee	$45 to $60 per week
Registered nurse days	$270 per month	Handyman	$54 per week
Proofreader	$65 to $70	Heating engineer	$8000 per year
Restaurant hostess	$55		
Dietitian	to $300 per month	Pharmacist	$100 per week
Market research	$70	Porter, office cleaning	$45 per week
Male:			
Fire adjuster	$3600 per year		
Elevator construction superintendant	$10,000 per year		
Wall Street cashier	$5200 per year		

● Supermarket Prices (A & P),
   1956

	Per pound		Per pound
Chicken	39¢	Jane Parker cherry	
Chuck steak	43¢	pie	39¢
Leg of lamb	55¢	Jane Parker	
Sirloin or		pumpkin pie	49¢
porterhouse	79¢	Jane Parker apple	
Shoulder of lamb	33¢	pie	53¢
Pork chops, center		Fruit cake, 3	
cut	69¢	pounds	$2.75
Veal chops, loin	89¢	Burry's chocolate	31¢ for 8¾
Jumbo Shrimp	99¢	chip cookies	ounces
Asparagus	17½¢		
Bananas	13½¢	Kellogg's Rice	25¢ for 8½
		Krispies	ounces
Muenster cheese	49¢	Wheatena	30¢ for 22
Swiss slices	74¢		ounces
Sharp cheddar	66¢	Quaker Oats	17¢ for 20
Nabisco Ritz			ounces
crackers	31¢	Post's Sugar Crisps	15¢ for 6
Ronzoni spaghetti	18½¢		ounces
Borden's milk	43¢ per half		
	gallon	Brillo Soap Pads	39¢ for two
Broccoli	21¢ per		packs of
	bunch		twelve
Corn	25¢ for four	Scottissue	53¢ for five
	ears		rolls
Iceberg lettuce	19¢ per head	Facial tissues	10¢ for box
Florida grapefruit	39¢ for five		of 200
	pounds	Tide, giant size	69¢
Sweet peas (can)	37¢ for two	Windex	35¢ for 20
	17 ounce		ounces
	cans	Scotkins dinner	
Del Monte fruit	47¢ for two	napkins	23¢ for 50
cocktail	17 ounce		
	cans		
Navel oranges	49¢ for ten		

● Highest Corporate Net Incomes, 1956

General Motors	$503 million
Standard Oil, New Jersey	$392 million
American Telephone & Telegraph	$300 million
U.S. Steel	$208 million
DuPont	$187 million
Creole Petroleum	$158 million
Gulf Oil	$138 million
Texas Co	$138 million
Ford Motor	$131 million
Socony Mobil	$124 million
Standard Oil, California	$122 million

● Auto Prices, 1956

Studebaker 2 door Sedan	$1597
Pontiac Catalina	$2658
Buick Special	$2395
Chrysler sedan	$2495
Chrysler New Yorker	$3095
Oldsmobile 88	$2471
Ford	$1775
Buick four-door sedan lease:	$90 per month
Rental, Avis: from $5 a day plus 8¢ a mile, insurance included	

● Vacations/Travel, 1956

Miami Beach (per day in February):

Shore Club Hotel	$15
Versailles Hotel	$16
Ritz-Plaza Hotel	$16
Casablanca Hotel	$16
Algiers Hotel	$17
Roney-Plaza Hotel	$17

S.S. *United States*
Five days from New York City to Le Havre

First class	from $350
Cabin	from $220
Tourist	from $172

Flights (one-way)

TWA New York City to California	$80
National New York City to Havana	$70.50
Northwest Orient New York City to Tokyo	$587
New York City to Manila	$649
Eastern New York City to Miami	$50.50
New York City to Atlanta	$35.50
New York City to St. Louis	$41
New York City to Houston	$71.20

Prestige Cards

☞ Around the turn of the century an American sociologist coined the phrase "conspicuous consumption" to describe how the well-to-do engaged in quite visible forms of self-indulgence (clothes, homes, cars, and vacations) as a way of stating and reinforcing their elevated positions in society. Today this process has taken on an added refinement since we can now display in a public manner our ability to consume thanks to credit cards. Not the common credit cards, mind you, because just about "everyone" has them (VISA boasts around 118 million cardholders and MasterCard just over 100 million) but the prestige cards that have not been offered to every Tom, Dick, and Harry. There are a number to choose from, assuming that you qualify. Predictably most of these cards are "gold." MasterCard International offers one to *preferred* customers (which implies that there are other kinds—tolerated, unwelcome, unnecessary?) and American Express has issued its plastic gold card to over 3 million special people. Visa International has reserved its Premier Visa card for between 2 million and 3 million richly deserving patrons. And let's not overlook that which is more precious than gold—platinum. American Express will consider you for a platinum card if you have in each of the last two years charged a minimum of $10,000 yearly. The prestige cards come with fancier price tags, often about double the usual annual fees. The platinum card stands by itself with a $250 annual fee. And interest rates on these credit card balances are just as lofty, averaging around 20 percent. But all of these charges matter little when, armed with your prestige cards, you are able to demonstrate to all around that you are a conspicuous credit card carrier.

Price Fixed

☞ We've all learned to roll with price increases. They advance, we grumble and consider doing without, but in the end our will usually succumbs to our wants. Not always, however. We do at times draw the line. Call it defiance, self-assertion, principled behavior, even nostalgia, we rise up to resist. When we do, it is because we recall the prices of certain items from our younger days, for products used frequently, enjoyed regularly. They vary from person to person, but this recent compilation will be broadly appreciated. How many turn away from the 45¢ chocolate bar once available for a nickel or the 10¢ ice cream pop now priced near a dollar? Who can eat hot dogs with the same abandon now that they cost over a dollar each, when the pleasure was once yours for 5¢? Who will stay home rather than part with $5 or more for a movie once a 25¢ treat or puff on a 10¢ cigar now on the counter for a dollar? Men's shoes, shoeshines, topcoats, a new car, a newsstand magazine—all may be passed up for violating an inbred sense of price fairness. No matter that our income has grown rapidly as well, probably outdistancing price advances. Certain things, not always easily affordable back then, nonetheless have become a part of our lives. As they are forever fixed in our memories so we wish them to remain in the marketplace.

The Price Is Right

☞ You expect in most any store today to see a price marker attached to each individual item. (It is an annoyance for most of us when it is not.) Often enough you'll know the cost beforehand. It may even have been that price, well advertised, that brought you into that particular store. The price as marked on the item is, you understand, what you will be asked to pay (unless you can demonstrate mislabeling or a failure to calculate the full discount). There is no haggling, no bargaining with the shopkeeper. (That is a diversion, such as it is, now available principally to vacationers on overseas shopping adventures.) Shoppers today will find this presentation quite elementary. The point, however, is that this most familiar of arrangements represented a major merchandising innovation when introduced over a hundred years ago.

Making bold use of the fixed, public price was the brainchild of one F. W. Woolworth. And it all happened in his five-and-ten-cents stores. If, he reasoned, people knew what the prices of everything were, in this instance either 5¢ or 10¢, they might come in (lured initially by attractive window displays) just to look, to browse, but might then decide to purchase. This you'll recognize as the beginnings of impulse buying. There need not be any interchange with sales personnel, certainly no bargaining nor undue pressure on people, except what they imposed on themselves. ("At 5¢ why not buy it? I might need it sometime.") In fact Woolworth reduced the sales staff in his stores and paid little to those remaining (at the beginning, $1.50 a week). No need, he insisted, for experienced salespeople because the goods, all priced and priced right, sold themselves. Not all the time, however. People had first to be drawn to and recognize them. Thus there came about a new interest in packaging and after that in advertising and brand recognition. But that clearly is a whole other story.

The Priceless Child

☞ As the cigars are handed out and congratulations are offered and accepted, inevitably someone asks, perhaps inappropriately, "Do you have any idea what that baby is going to cost you?" Of course you don't, but there are some people who claim to know, in fact have performed the necessary calculations. And the figures they offer are not in the least encouraging. Assuming you are aware that the latest research estimates that a kid will cost upward of $232,000 (for a child born in 1981, up to age seventeen), why in heaven's name go ahead and knowingly put yourself into such a bind? That is precisely the question addressed in a fascinating book entitled *Pricing the Priceless Child* by Viviana Zelizer (Basic Books, 1985). Part of the answer is to be found in the very title of the book. The child has become ever so precious and "priceless." Whatever the costs of raising him or her to adulthood, most families will accept the economic burden in return for the anticipated emotional satisfactions that accompany the process. That point of view is quite modern, surfacing only toward the end of the nineteenth century. Until then an entirely different outlook prevailed. For countless centuries children had been considered good investments. So it followed that the more you produced the better off you'd be. At an early age (four to five) they could be put to work around the house. Helping to cultivate the soil then followed in short order. By ten or twelve they qualified as full-fledged working members of the household, their contributions essential to the well being of the family unit. They would, years later, once again occupy a pivotal position, this time seeing to the support and comfortable old age of their parents. Such expectations still prevail in a good many places in the world. In the United States, however, a transformation occurred, according to Professor Zelizer, during the last quarter of the nineteenth century. By 1930 the new order was in place. We all live under it now, though it's unlikely we appreciate just what happened. Let's take a look. The child once viewed as a good investment, expected to work early on and contribute substantially, became the object of an entirely different set of expectations. No longer was he or she expected to be useful. They would no longer work (child labor laws saw to that) and contribute to the economic well being of the family. In fact they were given, indeed they expected, money (an allowance) just for being the child in the family. Rather than a producer, the child turned toward being a consumer. Parents took pride in what they could give to the child, how well they could support the little one. In return parents looked to the child for affection, love, and emotional dividends. That was to be the principal payoff. The child, now economically useless (indeed a notable drain), had become emotionally priceless. For a most compelling illustration of this point notice that as the child became economically useless he or she rose sharply in market value. (In the nineteenth century you had to pay someone to take your unwanted baby.) In fact childless couples are willing to pay more and more to obtain a baby. Prices for babies (especially on the black or gray market) have risen sharply. In the 1930s $1000 sufficed, whereas by the 1940s $5000 payments were common. In the early 1950s the price had risen to $10,000 and by the 1970s to $25,000. Today the figures on occasion even go higher. Yes, children contribute little economically (often when children work today we tend to assume that parents are exploiting them), consume inordinate amounts of our time, energies, emotions, and resources, and yet we go on having them (once more in increasing numbers). And this has happened amidst a people supposedly shrewd, calculating, materialistic. In this instance, however, the Almighty Dollar has yielded to the cute cuddly child, the Precious Baby.

The Price of Extinction

☞ For a price the marketplace will always provide, however rare the commodity or unauthorized the activity. Take the illegal trafficking in endangered animal species today. Whether sought after as pets, trophies, or for craft purposes or medicinal ingredients, various animals will appear in defiance of national and international laws. That's largely because profit margins can border on the spectacular. Follow, for example, the macaw parrot once it's caught by a Bolivian and offered to a trader for the equivalent of between 5¢ and 10¢. It's then sold to an exporter for $50, who in turn makes a deal with a US importer who pays $100 for the bird. The importer then closes a deal with a pet store owner for $1000, who then finds a customer happy to pay $2000. Prices for other illegal birds have soared, including the colored hyacinth macaw ($12,000), galah ($5500), the European goshawk ($2500 a pair), and the palm cockatoo ($8000 to $15,000). The gyrfalcon, much prized in falconry, reputedly has sold for $120,000 each in European and Middle Eastern markets. Back home, Indian warbonnets made of bald eagle feathers may bring up to $5000.

Two-legged animals continue to market rare species of the four-legged variety. Skins are generally in demand, such as those of the jaguar ($6000), or it may be body parts (note the paw pads of a grizzly bear, a dining delicacy at $150 a meal), or internal organs (again the grizzly, whose gallbladder, regarded by Asians as an aphrodisiac, will bring $5000), or external appendages, notably horns (elk antlers sell for $42 an ounce while the whole front rhino horn can bring $45,000). Head and shoulder trophies have been perennial favorites. In the United States fees for illegal hunts may go up to $7500, or if that proves inconvenient, trophies of bighorn sheep, elk, mountain goats, or deer can be yours for the vicarious thrills they bring at $20,000 each. (Consider trophies of the four types of wild sheep recently quoted at $50,000 for the grouping.) At these prices will not the distance between an endangered and an extinct species become progressively shorter?

Quiz Number 9

1. In 1937 _____ received the highest salary in baseball.
   a) Carl Hubbell b) Hank Greenberg c) Lou Gehrig d) Mel Ott

2. The total ring earnings of Sugar Ray Leonard were reported to be in excess of _____ million.
   a) 30   b) 10   c) 18   d) 45

3. After the first year, the average gross receipts of a McDonald's is _____.
   a) $675,000 b) $3.1 million c) $2.2 million d) $1.2 million

4. Of the doctors listed below _____ earn the most money.
   a) pediatricians b) radiologists c) psychiatrists d) internists

5. The US ambassador to _____ draws the highest salary.
   a) Brazil   b) Yugoslavia   c) Mexico   d) Hungary

6. In 1984, annual fuel costs for passenger cars totaled _____.
   a) $80 billion b) $18 billion c) 31 billion d) $50 billion

7. In February 1986 the Los Angeles Dodgers conducted the ultimate Adult Baseball Camp featuring five days of instruction with sixteen members of Baseball's Hall of Fame. Cost of the program was _____ per person.
   a) $2500   b) $1895   c) $3500   d) $4995

8. Among major family expenses from 1974 to 1984, _____ increased the most.
   a) tuition at a public college   b) a new house   c) a new car   d) private college tuition

9. A survey indicated that in 1984 average discretionary spending by college students came to _____ per month.
   a) $400   b) $125   c) $200   d) $600

10. Women are currently purchasing _____ out of every ten cars. a) one b) two c) three d) four

The Price of Life

☞ Life is precious, life is cheap. You'll find proponents for each of these points of view. Which one is correct? It depends. Philosophers may argue that life is monumentally precious and of infinite value, but in our marketplace society we tend to put specific value on things and even on people. (It's not only criminals who have a price placed on their heads.) The price varies considerably depending on circumstance and particular frames of reference. A surrogate mother will charge about $10,000 to bear the child of another couple, while hit men ask anywhere from $2500 to $10,000 and up to perform their nasty business. The chemical elements in the human body may be worth only about $8.37 but that's surely not a consideration when a boat sinks and the coast guard dispatches vessels and aircraft and spends tens of thousands of dollars in its search efforts. A family can sue a doctor for wrongful birth when recommended birth control measures fail. What will it now cost to raise and educate that child? There are lots of numbers around, none of them modest, all in the six-figure range. A severely damaged newborn can be kept alive at the cost of many thousands of dollars. Similar costs are involved when a very sick and elderly person is placed on life support systems. But then how explain the long-standing reluctance of the auto industry to install $800 seat bags which would save thousands of lives? The value of a human life therefore depends upon who is paying. If you are willing to pay higher insurance premiums you can get the price up to $50,000, $100,000, or $1 million easily enough. Die accidentally and suddenly you may be worth double the amount. (Worth more dead than alive may not misstate the situation.) You can be worth more if you're young and an earner. Then if you depart the earth it becomes a question of calculating what you would have earned over the normal span of life (including promotions and other pay increases). What you're worth may simply turn on a rather arbitrary figure devised by bureaucratic whim. Because the federal government stipulates that regulations reflect cost benefit considerations, agencies are obliged to assign a value to human life to determine the feasibility of new health and safety regulations. So, for example, OSHA (Occupational Safety and Health Administration) places the figure anywhere from $2 million to $5 million, whereas the Environmental Protection Agency sets it at about $1 million to $2 million and the Federal Aviation Administration at $650,083. What happens to proposed changes costing more than these figures per individual life saved? They're not done, which means that some of us will as a result be done for. Such realities certainly give one pause. You may at times look like a million bucks, but there's just no telling what price tag you'll carry.

Prime Times

☞ Few understand better than network television sales executives that time is money. The "time" in question is thirty seconds (though you see fifteen-second spots as well), and it is for sale—twenty-four such packages per prime time (between 8:00 and 11:00 P.M.) hour—to major corporate advertisers. Despite the fact that inflation has leveled off at between 3 percent and 4 percent TV prime time rates will rise 14.2 percent. You'll pay dearly for the privilege of appealing to the mass market. According to *Advertising Age* thirty-second prime time ad rates for the fourth quarter of 1985 averaged $118,840. But that figure tells only part of the story. Ask to place your ad on one of the hit shows and a different set of numbers comes into play. On Thursday evening at 8:00 NBC is sitting pretty with "The Cosby Show," charging about $270,000 for a thirty-second spot while ABC is forced to settle for $85,000 per slot on "The Fall Guy." Even when "The Cosby Show" signs off, enough people stay with NBC and its next show, "Family Ties," to enable the network to charge $220,000. Meanwhile CBS is offering "Magnum, P.I." at the same time and pocketing a relatively paltry $110,000.

Traditionally the biggest revenue producing nights are Thursday and Sunday. As it now stands NBC and CBS will battle to a draw here (recognizing that on Sunday CBS has the advantage of an additional prime time hour; the perennially popular "Sixty Minutes" is broadcast between 7:00 and 8:00). After "The Cosby Show" and "Family Ties" NBC's Thursday night lineup continues with "Cheers" ($175,000), "Night Court" ($155,000), then an hour of "Hill Street Blues" ($155,000). On Sunday evening CBS leads off with its blockbuster "Sixty Minutes" ($195,000), then offers three hour-long shows, "Murder She Wrote" ($130,000), "Crazy Like a Fox" ($125,000), and "Trapper John, M.D." ($115,000). If all the time slots sell out (and disregarding various advertiser discounts), there will be a standoff for top single night revenues between the two networks.

"Dynasty" reigns as king of the nighttime soaps ($235,000) with "Dallas" ($195,000) positioned as its closest challenger. The rest of the soaps check in the following order: "Hotel" ($175,000), "Knots Landing" ($175,000), "Falcon Crest" ($135,000), and "Dynasty II" ($130,000). The most expensive movie slot belongs to the ABC "Sunday Night Movie" ($145,000). Honors for the poorest one-night prime time performance seem to belong to CBS and its Wednesday night fare. For the first two hours neither "Stir Crazy," "Charlie & Co.," nor "George Burns' Week" will break into the six-figure column.

Do these exceptional ad rates mean anything to prime time viewers? Only that they can expect to see the same commercials presented by the same companies again and again. Who other than these giants can afford the costs of prime time exposure? Such repetition will make it all the easier to turn away from the TV set during the commercials. So why then are companies paying so much to reach the "viewing" audience?

Prize Packages

☞ To win a prize is fine but 'tis sweeter still if there is money besides. Remember Charles Lindbergh gained enduring fame

flying across the Atlantic, but his eye was on the $25,000 prize he stood to pocket. The Nobel Prize represents the supreme accomplishment of a lifetime, but that's no reason to downplay the $225,000 that currently goes with the award. If architecture is your field it would certainly be worth pursuing the $100,000 Pritzker Architecture Prize. The Albert Einstein Peace Prize, should you receive it, will be worth $50,000, a sum likely to itself enhance peace of mind. The MacArthur Foundation has on many recent occasions shown its willingness to commit up to $300,000 of its funds (over a period of five years) to talented individuals. The Albert Lasker Medical Prize carries the healthy sum of $45,000 while Washington college in Maryland confers the Sophie Kerr Award, an undergraduate literary prize worth a surprisingly beneficent $35,000. Then there are the high prestige, low payoff awards. The Pulitzer Prizes are good examples, bringing with them but $1000 checks (originally $500), as are the Obie Awards for off-Broadway theater ($1000). Of course most major awards quickly convert into financial benefits. Hollywood's Oscars certainly work that way. The recording industry operates a bit differently. When it awards gold and platinum records for exceptional sales volume, it rewards individuals who have already reaped substantial financial returns. The moral of the story is when in pursuit of a prize, compete for one that offers both a handshake and a hefty handout.

Pursuit of Wealth

☞ How are we to regard money and riches? Is the acquisition of wealth the be-all and end-all of our lives? Is the pursuit of money a universal craving or are we Americans merely deluded, manipulated victims chasing after unworthy objectives, victims of a false god? Expect an argument over this one. It's been raging unresolved ever since mankind managed to produce a surplus and arrange for its distribution. By now positions are fairly well established. For every detractor count a booster, for every cynic a true believer. Then add those who manage to combine both points of view.

Those more attuned to the spiritual have always doubted the importance of the material. Timothy's New Testament statement says it all: "The love of money," he warns us, "is the root of all evil." Nor are the wealthy especially worthy in God's eyes. "If," one observer declares, "you would know what the Lord God thinks of money, you have only to look at those to whom he gives it." Some have come to regard money as an unwelcome burden almost in direct proportion to the sums accumulated. Did not Ben Franklin warn eighteenth-century readers that "he who multiplies riches, multiplies care"? Who has not heard that "money can't buy happiness"?

A diversion, unworthy of serious attention, so naturalist Louis Agassiz regarded it. Rejecting an offer, he explained that "I cannot afford to waste my time making money."

There are an abundance of witnesses for the defense. It's hard to say it better than the Greek adage, "Money makes the man" or be more inclusive than George Bernard Shaw, who insisted that "money is the most important thing in the world." Be wary of any contrary view, writer Joyce Carol Oates warns: "The only people who claim that money is not important are people who have enough money so that they are relieved of the ugly burden of thinking about it." Thinking about it, especially when you don't have it, is a sure prescription for anxiety. Sean O'Casey recognized this when he observed that money "does not make you happy but it quiets the nerves." Let's leave the final word on this point to entertainer Sophie Tucker: "I have been poor. I have been rich. Rich is better."

No one disputes the power of money. The Reverend Ike insists his congregants understand that "money is God in action." Long before this writer Washington Irving had similar thoughts in mind when he wrote of "The Almighty Dollar." Who will deny that money talks and that people listen? "A rich man's joke is always funny" is confirmed by the view that "no matter how much money talks, most people don't find it boring." But *Fiddler on the Roof*'s Tevye said it best: "When you're rich they think you really know."

Thus the lines are drawn, the accounts not yet settled. And so it will remain.

Renting

☞ Are you bent on buying or would you rather rent? Today the choice is yours, though a good many people probably don't realize that. Nevertheless the range of rental items continues to grow, often in unexpected directions. All of us have done some renting besides an apartment. There have been rental cars, a tuxedo rental or two, maybe even a rented gown, a Halloween costume, and rented skis; then perhaps a rented wheelchair and crutches, but household furniture or a baby's playpen, a microwave oven, a bulldozer, or a dance floor? Not very likely. Still these and hundreds of other seemingly improbable items are readily available. Check out your local rental lenders. They're pretty much like department stores except that here *everything* gets returned.

Having a party? Rent it all. If you're planning to be outdoors and the forecast is for rain, rent a tent ($300 to $600, depending on size). Put a dance floor in ($22 for a 3' × 6' section) and a bubble machine for atmosphere ($16). Of course you'll need a bar ($25) and quite possibly a microwave oven ($31). Inside the

house it might get a bit stuffy, so play it safe and rent an air conditioner ($28). If you're catering mostly to kids, consider a loaner helium tank. For $19 you'll get gas enough for fifty balloons. For $60 the entire premises will float away or you can fill up 550 balloons. Then there are any number of costumes available. Assuming you're partial to Sesame Street you can fill the shoes of the Cookie Monster or Big Bird for $40 each.

Rentals are for special occasions. For a visitor arriving for a week a folding bed will do nicely ($20). The grandchild has been deposited in your house, now totally unequipped for such miniature inhabitants. No need to rack your brain, just rent. A highchair at $11 a week, a crib for $22, a playpen for $20, and a car seat ($12) will quickly make you feel young again.

People will occasionally rent equipment they already own. Icy or snowy weather usually leads to an upsurge in rented cars by people unwilling to take chances with their own vehicles. Chain saw owners may still rent when they face a job potentially damaging to their own equipment. Some homes contain little beyond the bare essentials. How else explain the rental of such pedestrian items as hammers and screwdrivers? As the purchase price of certain items rises, their rental potential grows. Lawnmowers provide a good example of this relationship. Assuming a good new lawnmower will cost about $300 you can rent one that works for $8 an hour. Use it ten or twelve times a summer and come out ahead for quite some time. While you're tending to your property you can also rent edgers, rototillers, post hole diggers as well as chain saws ($24 for four hours) and to clean up all the debris a bulldozer ($180 for the day). Should you happen to fall in love with any of the rented equipment, instead of returning it you can in many instances arrange for its purchase and the start of a more enduring relationship. Otherwise rest assured that whatever the item, if it is reasonably useful it can be readily rented.

Retiring Presidents

☞ "Golden parachutes" have provided business executives with soft, comfortable landings when they have chosen to leave the corporate hierarchy or have been ousted. Many of our presidents, however, have not fared nearly as well. They were once simply cut adrift and expected to fend for themselves. Some time ago we decided that was no way to treat former chief executives, and made provisions for their retirement years. Let's see just what they're entitled to and what our three ex-Presidents Nixon, Ford, and Carter are costing us. While in office they received salaries of $200,000 a year. Today their pensions bring each of them $82,438 annually and they still qualify for office expenses including postage of about $9000 each (Could they be writing that many letters?), telephone bills (ranging from Nixon's $20,000 charges and Carter's $21,000 tab to Ford's $30,000 total) and staff expenses ($100,000 each). Throw in some travel expenses (Ford $21,000, Nixon $11,000, and Carter $1183 in 1984). Yet all the amounts are still

AURORA '85

paltry compared to the costs of providing for their security. They're still prime targets for any would-be kidnappers or terrorists, so add on over $10 million for Secret Service protection for all three (though it ended for Amy Carter at age sixteen, and Nixon chose to drop it). Something new has been added to the presidential legacy: libraries with the government footing some part of the bill for these collections of presidential documents and memorabilia ($14 million in 1984). So you see we no longer neglect our ex-leaders. In addition publishers offer them lucrative book contracts so we can read their version of the facts, and they receive hefty payments for speaking engagements so that in the event we didn't read their account we can still hear their side of the story.

Royalties

☞ It's been quite some time since royalty had things its way. One monarch, however, managed a highly successful comeback thanks in large part to the full support and patronage of the common folk. That potentate was the King of Siam, a/k/a Yul Brynner, who first put on the crown and royal regalia back in 1951 when Rodgers and Hammerstein's *King and I* opened on Broadway. As a despot at times benevolent, Brynner ruled absolutely during his thirty-four-year association with the show. Not one to abdicate his position, he performed the royal role 4,625 times, which included three Broadway runs. His last and final engagement was a triumph. Tribute poured in from his loyal subjects and the king's coffers swelled marvelously. During the show's last week it set a Broadway box office record (with a one week's gross of $605,546 helped along by a $75 top price for the final performance). Reportedly Brynner amassed $8 million during this last reign on Broadway, a royal sum indeed. Though Yul Brynner is gone from our midst, the magnitude of this achievement will be remembered.

Quiz Number 10

1. Women who work full time have median incomes_____
   that of men.
   a) 82 percent b) 74 percent c) 91 percent d) 66 percent

2. A jumbo jet being built for King Fahd of Saudi-Arabia will
   reputedly cost_____.
   a) $35 million b) $75 million c) $325 million d) $150 million

3. The average IRS refund in 1985 was_____.
   a) $110   b) $1125   c) $475   d) $800

4. The typical Cadillac or Lincoln limousine sells for_____.
   a) $39,000 to $49,000   b) $22,000 to $28,000
   c) $50,000 to $55,000   d) $56,000 to $62,000

5. Golden parachutes usually refer to_____.
   a) supplementary pensions   b) air force awards
   c) skyjumping medal   d) executive compensation

6. During the Great Depression Babe Ruth received some
   criticism for his_____a year salary.
   a) $42,000   b) $80,000   c) $110,000   d) $62,500

7. The highest paid medical specialty is_____.
   a) oncology   b) radiology   c) neurosurgery
   d) anesthesiology

8. Bullet-proof vests cost_____.
   a) $175   b) $450   c) $700   d) $1125

9. A gold record album indicates sales of at least_____
   albums.
   a) 100,000   b) 1 million   c) 500,000   d) 750,000

10. In 1970_____received the highest salary in baseball.
    a) Tom Seaver   b) Pete Rose   c) Roberto Clemente
    d) Willie Mays

☞ *Answers:* 1) d; 2) d; 3) d; 4) a; 5) d; 6) b; 7) c; 8) c; 9) c; 10) d.

Scholarships

☞ An Ivy League education, they say, is like money in the bank, but of course such payoffs come only after graduation. Money first must flow out of that bank, sizable chunks of it in fact, to pay for some of the most expensive college years around. You're talking about $15,000 a year in base costs before "extras" like transportation, clothes, books, furnishings, and entertainment are considered. A scholarship would do nicely, but what if your kid is neither a genius nor a genuine candidate for the Heisman Trophy? And what if you're like most parents of Ivy Leaguers, comfortable? (With what you *have*, not with what you *owe* for it.) All is not lost according to the admissions office of at least one Ivy League institution, Dartmouth. Scholarship monies are available no matter what the income level. About one-third of the class of 1989 (356 out of 1024) came away with financial assistance of varying amounts. In those instances where family income fell below $10,000 annually, eighteen students received scholarships averaging $9510 each (the balance for tuition, and room and board would come from student jobs and loans). Families whose incomes ranged between $20,000 and $30,000 (and where other assets were modest) were expected to contribute approximately $2855 a year while Dartmouth offered seventy such students an average of $7995 a year in scholarship money. Nor was some relief denied to those solidly middle class families earning between $30,000 to $40,000. The children of eighty such families received an average of $6705 a year in scholarship money while their parents were expected to put up $4220 in each of four years. Not all upscale families are alike, said Dartmouth, for it awarded eleven scholarships where income exceeded $70,000. An average of $3250 went to these needy affluents. In short, a goodly number of students found Dartmouth, otherwise known as the Big Green, to be uncommonly generous with the green. And to those who paid full freight, remember, you can in time bank on an Ivy League education.

Short End

☞ Taxpayers shortchange the IRS. Students default on federally backed loans. Defense contractors cheat the government. Is Uncle Sam an easy mark, a soft touch? Is he always left holding the bag? It would seem so. Here's further evidence. It concerns many convicted criminals who are sentenced and also fined but then never pay the fines. At best the federal government collects about 55¢ of every dollar of fines imposed. Problem is no one in government takes responsibility and makes the effort to collect. Then again it is no simple task getting on a long line with other creditors or cutting through layers of camouflage and confusion to get at money well concealed. Frustration is mounting. There is even talk of legislation making nonpayment of fines a criminal offense!

Signs of the Times

☞ Many people consider them a blight on the landscape. To others they are an occasional source of amusement, a break in the monotony of highway driving. In cities they become part of the clutter that characterizes the urban environment. We're talking of course about billboard advertising. If the medium is the message, their impact must be substantial. (Standard sizes include 12' × 24', 14' × 40', and 20' × 60'.) Advertisers rent these outdoor displays by the month or by the year, and may either rotate a series of ads or stay with just a few. (Cigarette, alcoholic beverage, and auto ads tend to dominate.) Every space that may be within the sight lines of passing motorists becomes fair game (although highway beautification legislation and other restrictive ordinances are slowly reducing the numbers of outdoor signs, especially along interstate roadways). If there's no convenient surface at hand you've got to construct one, and that will cost you. In the South a typical 14' × 40' structure will set you back about

$35,000, a mere pittance compared to the $100,000 price tag in New York City. Now you have to devise a rate structure to justify the expenditure. Location is pivotal. A busy highway, especially one prone to tie-ups where drivers have little to do other than gaze at the display, is a most desirable location. (Traffic checks are performed periodically by audit bureaus to determine potential audience.) So is one where there are few if any other signs to compete for motorist attention. In the smaller towns monthly charges for a 14' × 40' billboard will range from $1500 to $2500. That same display in more populous areas will rent for $3500 to $4500 monthly. When it comes to spectacular outdoor displays few locations even come close to Times Square, New York. For decades the Great White Way has been home to the splashiest, most spectacular eye-catching open-air ads to be found anywhere. Square footage here is generous, as are some of the rental prices, which can range from $10,000 to $20,000 a month.

Before passing on, note should be taken of those very skilled and adventurous folks whose job it is Lilliputian-like to scale the heights and paste up the giant ad posters piece by piece. In New York at least, the efforts of these sign painters do not go unrewarded, with pay averaging $550 to $600 a week. One may not heed the messages they bring, but you cannot but appreciate the lengths to which they go to bring it to you.

Super Studs

☞ Horse players have forever reminded us of their higher calling—improving the breed. Now we're hearing that same explanation from the entire horse-breeding industry. Racing remains important but only as a tune-up for another sort of performance. You see, breeding's the thing these days. A horse needs to build a solid reputation out on the track but the real payoff comes not in the purse money but in the stud fees. The quicker the horse goes out to pasture the sooner the really big bucks can come rolling in. Little wonder owners are reluctant to continue racing their prize prancers. Horses may win some fat purses for sure, but they'll place themselves at risk of being injured (and possibly destroyed). And if they run they must be heavily insured, and that means colossal premiums. (It cost $2.2 million a year to insure 1978 Triple Crown winner Affirmed.) So the real race today is to syndicate top horses, that is, sell shares in them and offer purchasers the right each year to breed their horses with the reigning star. In recent years syndicate capitalization has reached impressive heights. Twenty-two million dollars flowed in for Affirmed, while Devil's Bag drew $36 million, Conquistador Cielo $36.4 million, and Sharif Dancer $40 million. Despite the sizable investment required, (for example, $900,000 to buy a share in Conquistador Cielo) handsome payoffs are possible. The first colt sired by Conquistador Cielo sold for $900,000 and it is expected his subsequent offspring will be auctioned off at an average price of $500,000. And should they perform well out on the track you can be sure future offspring will bring even higher prices. If, however, the horses finish out of the money consistently, bloodlines will be downgraded and even with lower stud fees suitors will become scarce. If they can't run there will be less fun for all.

Taking Stock

☞ It's just a seat and you're probably not going to do much sitting. Still it's well worth having, though just how much varies considerably. There aren't that many around (1,366) so to get one you're obliged to wait for someone willing to sell you his or hers. The whole undertaking started inauspiciously near the close of the eighteenth century (1792). Since then the New York Stock Exchange has grown to become the largest financial marketplace in the world. The seat entitles you to transact business out on the exchange. If you're ever offered one, grab it; otherwise be prepared to lay out considerable cash. When the market is on the move and the economic picture bright the price for a seat will reflect the buoyant optimism. In 1985, when the market seemed to catapult to new highs each day, the asking price for a seat

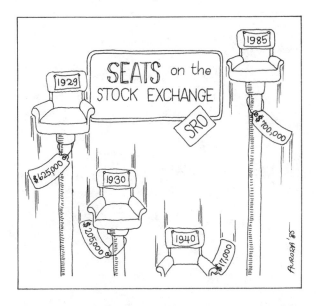

rocketed up by about $300,000 to over $700,000. Should a cooling off period set in, seat prices will likely moderate. The lowest selling price for a seat ($14,000), at least since the nineteenth century was recorded in 1896, a depression year. It never again sank to that level, although during the early years of World War II it came mighty close ($17,000). It's easy enough to guess when one of the highest seat prices was recorded. If you said 1929 you are correct, for in that year seats shot up to a high of $625,000. That's because there were plenty of stocks trading that year as annual volume reached the highest it had ever been (1.1 billion shares), a level not to be exceeded until the 1960s. Needless to say, the stock crash knocked not a few members out of their seats, and prices fell sharply. By the following year you could have picked one up for as little as $205,000, still a fair amount of cash. Predictably prices plummeted during the decade of the thirties and into the early war years. It would not be until the late 1950s that seat prices broke out over $100,000 again. Since then it has moved up and down but mostly up as the stock market has advanced to new highs amidst a huge trading volume. Recent prices have hovered between $425,000 and $475,000, so you'd best think twice before you pull up a seat and join the other exchange members.

1966

A war overseas and battles at home—we had seen better days. Demonstrations, confrontations, and riots became very much the order of the day. Was the violence of Vietnam backing up onto the American scene? Mounting casualties from the war and an increased commitment of American soldiers there meant rising monthly draft calls. More and more of America's youth would be caught up in that bloody struggle. While American B-52 bombers pounded targets in North Vietnam and along the demilitarized zone President Lyndon Johnson continued to pound home the theme that once North Vietnam halted its aggression the road to peace could be negotiated with ease. He labored mightily to maintain allied support for America's Southeast Asia policy although France's Charles de Gaulle, who had already removed French troops from NATO control, dissented and urged the United States to quit Vietnam. Much of the same thought could be heard from growing numbers of Americans as opposition to the war mounted. Antiwar demonstrations challenged millions of Americans, uncertain in their understanding of a conflict so remote and yet becoming so very close to home. President Johnson displayed no uncertainty. Opponents of the war were "nervous Nellies," detestable folk who were willing to turn on their leaders, on their country, and on its fighting men. That may have been enough to encourage counterdemonstrations by prowar groups. Such a volatile mix could explode at any time. War protesters came face to face with other Americans full square behind the president; and angry words, threats, and blows followed all too often (along with mounting evidence that right-wing "minutemen" groups were organizing, stockpiling weapons, and waiting for an opportunity to throw their weight around).

It's not possible to explain just why racial conflict flared up so violently, but it did. Almost always there was immediate provocation when all too often blacks were shot or roughly treated. It happened in the Watts section of Los Angeles, it happened when James Meredith attempted to walk the highways of Mississippi, it happened in Chicago and in so many other cities where violence flared up throughout the year. As blacks marched to give voice to their grievances and to demand meaningful changes, whites countermarched and counterdemonstrated. This pattern developed in Chicago where the Reverend Martin Luther King, Jr., had gone after his earlier civil rights efforts in the South. Campaigning for "open housing" he found himself vilified and assaulted by outraged white residents. Meetings with Chicago's Mayor Richard J. Daley offered few concrete results. The absence of observable change obviously had much to do with the rise of more militant black leaders no longer willing to accept the assurances or proceed with the caution of a Dr. King. The leadership of the Congress of Racial Equality (CORE) and the Students' Nonviolent Coordinating Council (SNCC) both endorsed "black power," stating openly that violence might prove necessary in the struggle. Black organizations such as the NAACP, Urban League, and the Southern Christian Leadership Conference (SCLC) repudiated or softened the implications of black power but many white Americans remained uneasy. "White blacklash" entered the vocabulary and the political stream. The Civil Rights Act of 1966 failed to pass and Congressman Adam Clayton Powell, Jr., an early advocate of black power, was all but stripped of his powers as chairman of the House Education and Labor Committee (specifically for absenteeism and other legal problems but also not unrelated to the charged racial atmosphere). Still and all the year saw a White House Conference on Civil Rights, the selection of Robert Weaver to a newly established Cabinet post as head of the Department of Housing and Urban Development (HUD)—the first black cabinet member ever—and the election in the fall of Senator Edward Brooke from

Massachusetts, the first black to enter the US Senate in the twentieth century.

In his State of the Union message delivered on January 12, President Johnson pledged that the United States would be able to meet its commitments overseas "while still building a Great Society here at home." A string of progressive measures followed. Legislation advanced the cause of cleaner water and allocated funds for housing the poor. Antipoverty programs expanded and President Johnson threw his support behind higher Social Security benefits and a boost in the minimum wage to $1.60 an hour. A bill mandating government funds for election campaigns became law, as did legislation assuring citizen access to information gathered and kept by government agencies (Freedom of Information Act). There would henceforth be more truth in packaging, and thanks to a campaign spearheaded by consumer activist Ralph Nader, more emphasis on auto and highway safety regulation. So things weren't all that bad after all. True, an American B-52 bomber had inadvertently dropped four H-bombs while flying off the coast of Spain early in the year, but American technology also made remarkable advances in space with the Gemini program and, back on earth, surgeons in Houston implanted an substitute heart in a human being for the first time. So you've got your choice of half full or half empty.

No such choice existed in the World Series. The heavily favored Los Angeles Dodgers came up completely empty, scoring but two runs in four games leading to a lopsided victory for Hank Bauer's Baltimore Orioles. The Orioles had previously taken the American League pennant by a comfortable margin of nine games. (The New York Yankees finished last, 26½ games behind.) The Dodgers, on the other hand, led by the incomparable Sandy Koufax, (who led the League in ERA for the fifth year in succession) just squeezed by their California rivals, the San Francisco Giants, to win the pennant. Among the outstanding performers of the season were Baltimore's Frank Robinson, who cracked 49 homers, batted .316 and drove in 121 runs; Hank Aaron of Atlanta, who led the National League with 44 home runs; and Pittsburgh's Matty Alou, who won the National League batting crown with a

.342 mark. The Most Valuable Player went to Robinson and to Roberto Clemente of Pittsburgh. Rookie honors were accorded to Tommy Helms of Cincinnati and Tommie Agee of the Chicago White Sox.

It was not a vintage year for America's tennis players. It was an all-Australian final in the US Open championship that saw Fred Stolle beat fellow countryman John Newcombe. Stolle then teamed with Roy Emerson to win the doubles crown. Wimbledon went to Spain's Manuel Santana, and the French, Italian, and Australian championships all went to the Aussies. On the women's side Maria Bueno of Brazil took the American singles crown, then teamed with Nancy Richey of the United States to capture the doubles title. Some American pride was salvaged when Billie Jean King won at Wimbledon. It was a different story among the golfers; the likes of Billy Casper, Jack Nicklaus, Don Massengale, Ken Venturi, Doug Sanders, Don January, and Arnold Palmer appeared repeatedly in the winner's circle. In the boxing ring it was the same story, at least in the upper weight divisions. Cassius Clay had little difficulty defending his heavyweight title against the likes of George Chuvalo, Henry Cooper, Brian London, and Karl Mildenberger. Jose Torres of New York remained king of the light heavyweights and New Jersey's Emile Griffith reigned as middleweight champ.

Football fans, especially the followers of professional football, had much to look forward to as the year came to a close. For the first time the champions of the upstart American Football League would do battle against the seasoned players of the venerable National Football League. The teams would meet in what was billed as the Superbowl. Earning their way into the postseason spectacular (by virtue of a 34–27 win over the Dallas Cowboys) were the powerful Green Bay Packers led by their quarterback, Bart Starr. Challenging the redoubtable Packers would be the Kansas City Chiefs, directed by quarterback Len Dawson. Whatever the outcome, the new venture into interleague competition would have a major impact on the fortunes of professional football. Also likely to have a major impact on a professional sport was Lew Alcindor, who led his UCLA Bruins teammates to the number one college basketball ranking in both the AP and UPI polls and would undoubtedly make UCLA the favorite in the postseason NCAA basketball tourney. Other college players attracting favorable notice included Jim Walker of Providence, Wes Unseld of Louisville, and Elvin Hayes of Houston.

George Plimpton made it into the ranks of pro football for a brief moment of glory, and told his story with great humor in his book, *Paper Lion*. Perhaps Plimpton may have just been releasing energies examined in the animal kingdom by Konrad Lorenz in his exceptional study entitled *On Aggression*. Far more destructive and horrific was the story told by Truman Capote in his memorable "nonfiction novel," *In Cold Blood*, a tale of murder out in Kansas. That other natural tendencies often take hold was well documented in the volume, *Human Sexual Response*, written by William Masters and Virginia Johnson, popularly known as the Kinsey Report of 1966. Fictionalized and unrestrained, these tendencies formed the theme of two of the year's best sellers, Harold Robbins's *The Adventurer* and Jacqueline Susann's *Valley of the Dolls*. Other more distinguished fiction included Bernard Malamud's *The Fixer*, Graham Greene's *The Comedians*, and Louis Auchincloss's *The Embezzler*. Fact or fiction was precisely the point raised by Edward Jay Epstein in *Inquest*, a provocative analysis that created doubts about the Warren Commission and its findings on the assassination of President John F. Kennedy.

Doubts about academicians were raised in what certainly was the most talked about film of the year, *Who's Afraid of Virginia Woolf?*, starring Elizabeth Taylor and Richard Burton. Nearly as provocative was *A Man for All Seasons* featuring Paul Scofield. It seemed as if everyone was attempting their own versions of James Bond. There was Dean Martin in *The Silencers*, James Coburn in *Our Man Flint*, and David Niven in *Where the Spies Are*. But Bond fans weren't taken in, not when they had the real 007 to watch in *Thunderball*. Quite a few foreign-made films gained distribution here and we were generally the better for it, especially since they included *Born Free, Alfie, Morgan*, and *The Sand Pebbles*. Two excellent comedies, *The Russians Are Coming, the Russians Are Coming*, starring Alan Arkin, and Billy Wilder's *The Fortune Cookie* kept moviegoers in a cheerful frame of mind. Broadway theatergoers did not appear to be as fortunate. Two holdovers, *Man of*

La Mancha and *Cactus Flower* did well, and *Sweet Charity, Mame,*
and *Wait until Dark* opened to generally favorable notices, but
Broadway had known and hopefully would have more distinguished and stimulating seasons.

ODDS AND ENDS IN 1966

• Employed individuals have $277.20 withdrawn from their pay-
checks for the first $6600 in income for Social Security.
• Secret Service reveals that counterfeiting reached an all-time
high. Agents recover $9 million in bogus bills. About 10 percent
of counterfeit currency went into circulation.
• Marvin Miller is named executive director of the Major League
Players Association at a salary of $50,000 a year.
• The guaranteed annual income for New York's longshoremen is
about $5500 a year.
• Greyhound bus drivers average $8000 a year.
• The minimum salary for nurses in New York is $5150 a year; for
garbage collectors, $5496.
• A New York City taxi driver averages $105 a week from com-
missions and tips.
• A German corporation agrees to pay $625 each to former con-
centration camp inmates whom the company used as slave labor
during Nazi regime.
• Federal minimum wage is $1.25 an hour.
• A jury in a New York State Supreme Court awards $200,000 to
a lawyer whose nose was bitten off by an angry litigant.
• As of November 1 Willie Shoemaker maintains his position as
the world's leading money-winning jockey with total winnings of
$37.3 million.
• The base salary for members of the National Symphony Orchestra, Washington, D.C., is $5840 per year.
• Summer camps for kids for an 8-week session range in price from
$425 to $750.
• Most recent statistics indicate hospital day rate was $30 in 1959,
$39 in 1963 and $41.58 in 1964.

• Disk jockeys on New York's WOR-FM agree to a minimum pay level of ̃$175 a week, a little less than half the salary paid on WOR-AM.

• The top established ticket price for a World Series game in Los Angeles is $12.

• Actor George Hamilton fends off questions regarding romantic attachment with Linda Bird Johnson but raises his asking price from $50,000 to $100,000 a movie.

• New York City pays the highest interest in thirty-four years on its recently issued bonds: 4.75 percent.

• The price of a haircut in Philadelphia rises to $2.25.

● Help Wanted Female, 1966	
Executive secretary	$125 *per week*
Bank clerk (experienced)	$125 *per week*
College girl	$85 to $100 *per week*
Housewife	$75 to $95 *per week*
Junior stenographer	$80 to $85 *per week*
Receptionist trainee	$68 to $75 *per week*
Clerk	$75 to $85 *per week*
Girl Friday	$75 *per week*
Girl factory trainee	$1.75 *per hour*
Girl to answer phone	$1.25 *per hour*
Colorist	$100 *per week in commissions*
IBM keypunch	$85 to $100 *per week*
Receptionist	$80 *per week*
Teach ballroom dancing	$3 to $5 *per hour*
Part-time housewife	$26 *for 8 hours*
Waitress, Greenwich Village	$1.50 *per hour*
Sleep-in maid	to $85 *per week*
Live-in houseworker	$65 *for 5½ days*
Housekeeper-cook, sleep-in	$75 *per week*

● Help Wanted Male, 1966	
Accounting clerk	$95 to $105 *per week*
Mailroom boy	$70 to $85 *per week*
Bank teller	$85 to $125 *per week*
Boy, cleancut, high school graduate	$75 to $80 *per week*
Guard	$86 to $126 *per week*
Hairdresser	$85 to $100 *per week plus commission*
Mail messenger	$55 to $65 *per week*
Print production assistant	$6500 *per year*
Programmer	to $180 *per week*
Electric typewriter mechanic	$9000 *per year*
Wall Street clerk	$95 to $140 *per week*
Supermarket manager	$190 *per week*
Building superintendent	$115 *per week plus apartment*
Gas station attendant	to $100 *per week*
Maitre d' country club	$150 to $175 *per week*
Movie manager trainee	$5200 *per year*
Photo retoucher	$175 to $250 *per week*

● Help Wanted Male, 1966

Travel agent	$125 *per week*	Personnel	$10,000 to
Washing machine serviceman	$150 *per week*	management	$13,000 *per year*
		Construction	to $16,000 *per*
Biology teacher M.S.	$7600 *per year*	engineer or architect	*year*
Computer sales trainee	$6000 to $7000 *per year*	Chemist, assistant director	to $20,000 *per year*
Production supervisor, plastics	to $9000 *per year*		

● Houses for Rent, 1966

Bungalow for rent for season on ocean.

Fire Island $800

Colonial farmhouse, three bedrooms, two baths, living room, dining room, kitchen, July 1 to Labor Day.

East Hampton, Long Island $2500

Modern tri-level, three bedroom, brand new, exceptionally beautiful, per season.

South Wellfleet, Massachusetts
$1500

● Houses for Sale, 1966

Forty-five acres, modern home, garage, barn suitable for ten horses Berkshire-Tanglewood asking
$37,500

Handsome English cape, stone and brick, living room with fireplace, separate dining room, new kitchen, four big bedrooms, two baths, screen porch, carpet, appliances, finished basement, two-car garage, low taxes, deadend street.

Great Neck, Long Island $34,500

Delightful split level cottage built in 1960. Cheerful rooms. Four bedrooms, two and a half baths, playroom. Fairly priced. Taxes $805.

Scarsdale, New York $35,500

● Houses For Sale, 1966

Twelve-year-old center hall
Colonial, excellent condition, large
living room, dining room, modern
kitchen, breakfast room, den, four
bedrooms, two and a half baths,
recreation room, three fireplaces.
    Scarsdale, New York $59,500

Yellow frame, two and a half story
Colonial, twelve years old. Eight
rooms, three and a half baths, four
double bedrooms, large screened
porch, library, garage for three
cars, located on one acre on gentle
knoll site, fringed by woodland.
    Greenwich, Connecticut $90,000

Directly on Long Island Sound,
modernized brick ranch, four
bedrooms, three baths, embracing
water panoramas from three
terraces. Swim, bask, fish.
    Darien, Connecticut $87,500

● Bowery Savings Bank Interest
  (New York City), 1966

Passbook Loan	5.43 percent
Secured personal loan	8.09 percent
Unsecured personal loan	10.07 percent
Revolving credit	12 percent

● Governors' Salaries, 1966

New York	$50,000
California	$44,100
Michigan	$40,000
Ohio	$40,000
Connecticut	$35,000
Massachusetts	$35,000
Pennsylvania	$35,000
Hawaii	$33,500

● Foundation Assets, 1966

Ford Foundation	$2.4 billion
Rockefeller Foundation	$854 million
Duke Endowment	$691 million
Kellogg Foundation	$491 million
Carnegie Foundation	$344 million

● Federal Income Taxes—After
  Standard Deductions and
  Exemptions, 1966

Income	Tax
$10,000	$1,820
$15,000	$3,010
$25,000	$6,020
$50,000	$17,060
$100,000	$45,180

● Hardcover Book Prices, 1966

Jacqueline Susann, *Valley of
    the Dolls* $5.95
Bernard Fall, *Vietnam
    Witness* $6.95
John F. Kennedy, *Profiles in
    Courage* $5
Bel Kaufman, *Up the Down
    Staircase* $4.95
Truman Capote, *In Cold
    Blood* $5.95
James Michener, *The Source* $7.95
Arthur M. Schlesinger, Jr.,
    A Thousand Days $9
Albert Camus, *Exile and the
    Kingdom* (Vintage
    Paperback) $1.65
E. Franklin Frazier, *The
    Negro Family in the
    United States* (Phoenix
    Paperback) $2.45

● Salaries of Federal Officials,
    1966

President $100,000
Vice-president $43,000
Cabinet member $35,000
Senator $30,000
Chief Justice $40,000

● College Tuition—Annual, 1966

Amherst $1500
Boston College $1400
Dartmouth $1925
Duquesne $1300
Holy Cross $1400
Johns Hopkins $1800
Michigan
    (resident of
    state) $348
Pennsylvania
    State (resident
    of state) $450
Radcliffe $1760
Sarah Lawrence $2350
Syracuse $1720
Texas (resident
    of state) $100
Yale $1950

● Total Value of Currency in
    Circulation, 1966

$13.5 billion	$20 bill
$8.2 billion	$100 bill
$7.8 billion	$10 bill
$3.5 billion	$50 bill
$2.5 billion	$5 bill
$1.8 billion	$1 bill
$134 million	$2 bill

● Toll Roads, 1966

	Maximum Toll
New York Thruway, 559 miles	$8.20
Kansas Turnpike, 236 miles	$4.95
Sunshine State Parkway, 265 miles	$4.80
Pennsylvania Turnpike, 360 miles	$4.80
Ohio Turnpike, 241 miles	$3.50
Massachusetts Turnpike, 135 miles	$3.00

● Automobiles, 1966 models

Plymouth Fury	$2020
Ford	$2348
Valiant two-door	$1815
Thunderbird	$3649
Rambler America	$1935
Ford Mustang	$2129
Simca	$1553
Datsun	$1599
Triumph TR-4A	$2820
Jaguar 4.2 sedan	$6864
Opel Kadett	$1644

● Entertainments, New York City, 1966

Ray Charles at Carnegie Hall	$3.00 to $6.00
Peter Nero at Philharmonic Hall	$2.75 to $4.95
Mark Twain Tonight	$2.00 to $6.00
James Brown Revue at Madison Square Garden	$2.50 to $6.00
New York Rangers v. Detroit Red Wings (Hockey)	$1.50 to $6.00
Pro Basketball doubleheader at Madison Square Garden	$2.50 to $5.00
Hello Dolly! on Broadway	$3.00 to $9.90
Barefoot in the Park on Broadway	$2.75 to $7.25
Cactus Flower on Broadway	$3.60 to $7.50
Fiddler on the Roof on Broadway	$2.80 to $9.10
The Sound of Music (movie), Rivoli Theatre	$2.00 to $4.25
Chicago Symphony at Carnegie Hall	$2.50 to $6.50

• Auto Rentals/Leases, 1966

Olins—$8.95 & up per day—no mileage charge	
Cadillac lease 26 months	$119 per month
Volkswagen lease 26 months	$49.99 per month
Impala lease 26 months	$94 per month
Bonneville lease 26 months	$134 per month, including maintenance
Riviera lease 26 months	$146 per month, including maintenance

Talk Shows

☞ Capture public attention, become a celebrity. Get well known (for just about anything). Now you're marketable and can be merchandised as readily as strawberry shortcake. Endorsements, promotions, personal appearances, book contracts, they're all yours if the flesh is willing and the timing is right. There's nothing to it, except the payoffs. They're impressive. The lecture circuit is vast as hosts of business organizations, convention planners, trade associations, and campus lecture bureaus are looking for names that will draw a crowd. Free speech is a fine principle but on the lecture circuit talk is not cheap. Take note of some record fees. (The college circuit pays well but not nearly as handsomely as bookings on the corporate-convention calendar.) G. Gordon Liddy of Watergate memory was until recently rattling about at $4000 a talk (until after about 400 college appearances, after sharing the stage with Timothy Leary, he finally became history and the market dried up). Ralph Nader has and will take up the cudgels for $5000, whereas Jack Anderson for $7000 will dispense his inside dope. Go left, go right, either John Kenneth Galbraith or William Buckley can be yours for $10,000. Political conservatives are benefiting liberally as pay for patter opportunities abound for them. Columnist William Safire ($12,000), economist Milton Friedman ($15,000), radio commentator Paul Harvey ($20,000), and Henry Kissinger ($20,000) are giving audiences what they want to hear. Political reruns are faring well of late. Jimmy Carter and Jeanne Kirkpatrick can come away with as much as $20,000 for having "been there," while Geraldine Ferraro ($17,500), Gerald Ford ($15,000 to $25,000) and the Rev. Jesse Jackson ($15,000 to $20,000) have no qualms about repeating themselves, so long as the lecture invitations keep coming. Television exposure does wonders for your ratings and rates, witness Walter Cronkite's top fee ($35,000 to $40,000) as well as those of Barbara Walters (up to $25,000), Ted Koppel ($20,000), Dan Rather ($20,000), and David Brinkley ($17,500). If they're out of your price range consider Carl Sagan at $15,000, Art Buchwald ($12,500), or Dr. Ruth Westheimer, whose campus comments usually start flowing for a $7000 minimum fee. Of course these rates and the top draws will vary with the ebb and flow of public events, the passage of time, and the arrival of new luminaries onto the circuit. So while the going is good, it's best to get talking.

Tennis Anyone?

☞ Tennis, it appears, has lost its bounce. Once-active players are heading for the sidelines. Back in 1976 the future looked rosy indeed when Americans bought 8.6 million rackets for $183 million. That turned out to be the record; purchases have dropped sharply since. In 1985 only 2.7 million rackets left the shops although revenues of $186 million were about the same as in 1976 due to the increased price of a racket (average $69 each). There's far more bounce to the golf business, which chipped in at $600 million in yearly sales, a level twice that of tennis. Compared to the sale of 2.7 million tennis rackets, 10.3 million sets of golf clubs moved out in 1984. Are we to conclude that Americans would rather walk than run?

That's Extravagant!

☞ An extravagance is wildly improbable, absurdly impractical, uniquely irrational, limited to periods of complete abandon, totally reckless consumption. Such a definition would find favor among Neiman-Marcus marketing executives who have, for the last twenty-five years, elevated the Neiman-Marcus extravagance into an annual happening. Each year a most uncommon his and hers gift item has found its way into the Neiman-Marcus Christmas catalog so that this upscale Dallas-based retailer could maintain its image as the mecca of lavish lunacy, Texas style. It all started with his and hers airplanes in 1960 for a combined price of $176,000, moving on two years later to thirty-foot Chinese junks ($11,500 each) to a fourteen-foot minisubmarine ($18,700) in 1963 and dirigibles ($50,000) in 1979. Animals have found their way into this select company on a number of occasions, including camels in 1967 ($4125), purebred buffalo calves in 1976 ($11,750), ostriches in 1980 ($1500), and Chinese Shar-Pei puppies ($2000), in 1983. Defying easy classification were the 2,000-year-old mummy cases ($16,000 each in 1971), the 1977 windmills ($16,000) and the robots for domestic duties ($15,000 in 1981). 1985 saw a return to the more conventional extravagance, diamonds. How unoriginal, except for their size and price. Both natural yellow diamonds, one was fifty-six carats, the other twenty-one, priced together for a sparkling $2 million. Orders for the above gifts are never very heavy, but that's the way it should be. Surely they're not for everyone.

Tips on Tipping

☞ Who started tipping people and ruining things for the rest of us? History probably won't help with this one. Anyway we're stuck with the system, though it's not one everyone understands. Prices are advertised and posted, while tips, though expected, are merely implied or suggested. Paying the stated price completes the transaction usually to the satisfaction of both buyer and seller, but with tipping you're never sure you've "paid" what was expected. But maybe that's part of the system, originally designed, no doubt, to distinguish the savvy insiders and sophisticates from the rest of the pack. The former know who, when, and how much to tip. The latter are awkward, puzzled, in obvious need of guidance. Should one tip the garbageman (yes, $10 to $20 at Christmas), newsboy ($5 to $10, same time of the year), letter carrier ($10 to $20, ditto, never mind federal law), and what about the hairdresser ($10 to $20 or food or liquor in addition to the regular handouts), the building superintendent ($25 to $50) and handyman ($10 to $20)? The average person may recognize tipping is in order but be unaware of the going rate. They probably realize coat check attendants merit a dollar a coat, but will they know the bartender expects to receive 15 percent to 20 percent of the tab? They'll want preferred seating at the restaurant but will wonder just how much of a tip to slip the maitre d' ($10 to $20). They'll feel uncomfortable seeing a washroom attendant, not knowing how much to leave (50¢ to $1), and will probably tip too much to the waiter for service that was erratic and unobliging (tips for waiters range from 15 percent to 25 percent in the large American cities). On the way home you can expect them to fumble for the cab fare and give an unnecessarily large tip probably because they didn't think to have small bills on hand or were too embarrassed to ask the cabbie for change.

Those who decry this awkwardness and uncertainty as a sign of the imminent decline and fall of our civilization are probably overreacting. Indeed some of it can be understood as a healthy and welcome indication of independence and of resistance to a system that puts a premium on intimidation and ostentation and creates favoritism and uncertainty. After all, does not "greasing the palm" create slippery conditions for all?

Quiz Number 11

1. In 1984 American workers earned an average of $9.17 while in Japan the figure was_____an hour.
   a) $8.23   b) $6.05   c) $4.50   d) $10.02

2. In the 1930s the average movie admission price for adults was_____.
   a) 10¢   b) 18¢   c) 25¢   d) 40¢

3. In early 1985 the average price for an acre of American farmland was_____.
   a) $2050   b) $697   c) $1471   d) $1040

4. The average cost of producing a major motion picture in the United States is_____million.
   a) 8.5   b) 6.1   c) 14.5   d) 19.1

5. The most profitable aspect of publishing is_____.
   a) children's books   b) art books   c) college textbooks
   d) paperbacks

6. Highest total advertising revenues are enjoyed by_____.
   a) television stations   b) newspapers   c) magazines
   d) radio stations

7. Of the American food dollar,_____goes for eating out?
   a) 18¢   b) 24¢   c) 30¢   d) 40¢

8. In 1954, the Dow Jones Industrial Average broke the 380 level, first set in_____.
   a) 1920   b) 1926   c) 1929   d) 1946

9. In 1984 of the following luxury cars,_____had the highest US sales. a) Mercedes   b) Audi   c) BMW

10. In 1984 construction costs per room to build a commercial class hotel were about_____.
    a) $22,000   b) $51,000   c) $74,000   d) $95,000

Traveling Light

AURORA '85

☞ A recent national survey by *Money* magazine revealed that on average Americans carried $27 in their wallets. Only $27 for a people among the richest on earth? Are budgets that tight or is it a question of habit or long-standing tradition? Could it be the fear of crime that keeps wallets thin? (You don't want to risk antagonizing a thief by carrying nothing. Twenty-seven dollars will anger but probably not infuriate.) Have credit cards and checks all but eliminated the need for having cash on hand, or don't people trust themselves to resist the impulse to buy?

Could the $27 figure be an error? We all know people who make a game out of getting through the day with the least amount of money possible, hoping perhaps to borrow from others, and of certain well-to-do folk who practice a reverse snobbery by taking little or no petty cash with them, but we also encounter those who delight in the large bankroll. Whether from a deprived upbringing, the need to feel secure, or a desire to impress others, these people are ever eager to flash the green. Any survey that includes them would yield figures well in excess of $27. So let's all empty our pockets and open our wallets. A recount is in order.

Tuition Blues

☞ Who hasn't heard tell of the plight of families with college-bound sons and daughters. Unless monies had been deposited almost from the day the infant was deposited into the bassinet, chances diminish that a cache sufficient to sustain four years of high college tuition payments can be accumulated beforehand. Yet there is another group of parents facing an even more formidable challenge. They are the ones who first chose to send their kids off to private prep schools. They face three years of school bills even before college tuition payments begin, surely an advanced stage of masochism.

Certain prep schools have long enjoyed the enviable position as feeders to the prestige undergraduate institutions, functioning as sort of a "headstart" program for the privileged. What does one pay for these preferred positions in the starting gates? Recent figures show relatively little variation among the better known schools (most all of which, not incidentally, are located in the Northeast, almost within walking distance of the Ivy League colleges and other prestigious institutions). St. Paul's in New Hampshire charges $9300 a year for tuition, room, and board; and most of the others stay within a few hundred dollars of that figure. Phillips Andover (Massachusetts) and Phillips Exeter (New Hampshire) check in at $9200–$9500 respectively. Deerfield Academy in Massachusetts and the Hotchkiss School in Connecticut set figures of $9100–$9500 while somewhat more costly are Groton (Massachusetts) at $10,200 and Miss Porter's School (Connecticut) at $10,200. The tuition title appears to belong to Lawrence Academy (Massachusetts), coming in at $10,600.

The way to bring costs down (short of withdrawing your child and sending him or her back to public school) is to select a nearby prep school, thereby eliminating room and board expenses. Attending New York's Chapin School for girls involves a $4600–$6500 tuition charge (depending on grade), the Dalton School $5100–$7300, while others show but slight variations. Running the tuition gauntlet of prep schools does have its consolations. Parents enjoy the status that comes with having their children attend prep schools and they gain early valuable experience in paying tuition bills. By the time the college bills come rolling in they are already old hands at making ends meet.

Tuition Terror

☞ By early spring high school seniors learn which colleges have accepted them. Shortly thereafter parents learn the precise costs of acceptance. In recent years automobile "sticker shock" has been replaced by "tuition terror" as the most fearsome menace stalking the middle class, especially with the annual publication of the collegiate tuition's top ten. Look for repeated appearances by Bennington, Massachusetts Institute of Technology, Harvard, Radcliffe, Princeton, Yale, Brown, Barnard, and Stanford. And look for spirited defenses of college charges beginning with the value-added argument that is usually expressed in the form of additional earnings over a lifetime. Expect to hear that tuition pays for but a portion of the costs, followed by the assertion that while costs are higher the burden, because of rising incomes, has not necessarily become heavier. Middle-aged parents who remember their college years costing less than one year's tuition today take little comfort in all this. Still the fact is that while college tuition has increased an average of 6.4 percent annually since 1961, family disposable income has gained by 7.7 percent. It's just that families are not keen on disposing of all their discretionary income in this manner, or accepting restrictions on their accustomed lifestyle.

(Recent studies show that 24 percent of college students come from households where the annual income is between $25,000 and $40,000 a year, 29 percent have families whose income falls between $40,000 and $50,000 annually, while 19 percent have parents earning $50,000 and beyond.)

Try running a college; it's not easy. One research economist who has been tracking the costs of 200 items typically purchased by colleges since 1961 (the Higher Education Price Index) notes that it has consistently outpaced the Consumer Price Index. Remember you have to keep the library open late and see to it that it's well lit. Equipment needs upgrading and replacement if you wish to operate a respectable, up-to-date program in the sciences. The computer revolution has brought new pressure on the colleges to keep pace. Then faculty salaries must be increased from time to time (though in fact the real income of academics has declined in recent years).

Private colleges would operate at a deficit were they to depend exclusively on tuition payments. According to its president, Bryn Mawr, for example, receives 60 percent of its revenues from tuition, and must rely on gifts (30 percent) and endowment funds (10 percent) to balance its annual budget. That means pampering alumni, catering to potentially substantial donors, and praying that the stock and bond markets continue their upward course. That's why tuition is becoming a larger factor in college budgets. This will continue as colleges consistently add a few percentage points to the annual Consumer Price Index to determine each year's tuition increase. But don't worry. Your life will be simpler for it. You'll not need to be concerned about spending discretionary income. Colleges are planning to dispose of it for you.

Umpires' Revenge

☞ Mike Schmidt of the Philadelphia Phillies slides into third, then protests vigorously when the umpire calls him out. It's all part of the game, but there is something almost inspirational here because

the umpire in this case is a rookie making $28,000; yet he still
has the last and final word with a ball player taking in $2.1 million
for working that same season. And so it goes throughout the major
leagues. Ball players' salaries have taken off (the average 1985
salary is $370,000) leaving most everyone else in the dust, umpires
included. Top salary for an umpire reaches $72,000 (all get $100
a day plus air fare for expenses). On the minor league level compensation remains shabby. (In class A ball it's $1300 a month. At
the Triple A level, the highest in the minors, umps get $1950 per
month for a five-and-a-half month season.) So next time you're
prepared to defend a high-priced ball player who is abusing a
modestly compensated umpire, understand why it is a case of
adding insult to injury.

Underground Economy

☞ To the IRS the underground economy is a source of envy and frustration. To moralists it suggests an increased spirit of lawlessness. Economists view it as a fascinating area for speculation and calculation. But to those involved it's just another way of making money or hanging on to more of what you have. If the network actually were "underground" it would be far less significant than it is. But in fact it operates out in the open within the "needle parks" across America in the neighborhood numbers games, in the flea markets and among the street peddlers, with the moonlighters paid off the books, the businessmen directing proceeds straight through into their pockets, and the taxpayers relentless about deductions, but strangely forgetful regarding income. It is not so much underground as unwritten and unaccounted for.

But if you talk to Donald (no last names here; you're surprised when he offers you his first, which may not of course be his real one), you'll find someone perfectly content with the way things are. Donald is a New York City street peddler (an itinerant merchant, is the way he characterizes himself). You'll find him in any number of locations, depending upon the time of day and season of the year. In the mornings and evenings, he indeed goes "underground" to sell his goods in subway stations during the rush hour. In the late morning and afternoon it's on to Midtown and a choice Madison Avenue location. On the weekends he moves to the Upper West Side and sets up outside a well known food shop.

He complains about business on this Sunday afternoon but then confesses he had an unusually busy morning. He is, on this summer day, selling an assortment of designer windbreakers, men's tops, and women's bathing suits. Maintaining a constant patter he coaxes the curious over to his three-carton curbside stand. Do the police worry him? Yes and no. They will, he concedes, confiscate all exposed goods when they come by. (They nab him in one place or another as often as once a week, costing him an

average $150 in goods.) As a result he is careful to display as few
pieces as he can, always poised, however, to whip out additional
items from the cartons upon request. On the other hand the police
make it difficult for the competition as well. Often, he hinted,
more difficult.

He gets most of his goods from one supplier who, because he
buys in quantity, allows him to pick and choose specific items
instead of insisting upon bulk lot purchases. He knows what customers want; what he selects, sells. It's all cash, leaving few if
any traces. Donald does accept checks and incredibly, despite his
street trade, has seen only a handful bounce over the past few
years. (He's especially proud of his work as collection agent, per-
sonally pursuing those who have passed rubber checks.) Is the
street trade worth all the effort? (Remember the inventory must
be moved about a few times each day.) There is no hesitation here.
"Two to three thousand dollars a week. Net!" Reacting to the
incredulous look he repeats it. "You have the right goods and this
stuff really moves. People here know prices. I'm beating everyone.
No lines, no hassle, no taxes. And if it's the wrong size, I'm here,
I'll take it back." One story out of a million from America's thriving
underground economy. Opportunity lives!

Wage Hikes

☞ Is there anyone holding a job today who doesn't expect pay
increases early and often? Each new contract, all increases in the
cost of living, every additional year of service, these are just some
of the usual justifications for higher pay. Not to receive an increase
is to fail. A wage freeze is unacceptable, is a fundamental violation,
a flagrant denial of normal expectations. In light of this, what is
one to make of the following slice of life taken from the mid-
nineteenth century, a period, one imagines, of robust growth?

What we have are daily wage rates for carpenters employed in
maintenance work on the Erie Canal. The records continue for

fifty-three years, and they reveal surprisingly stable levels of compensation. In 1820 these carpenters received one dollar a day for their services. True, ten years later wages had risen to $1.55, but in 1849 they were just $1.63, only an 8¢ advance in ten years. Labor shortages during and after the Civil War pushed the daily rate upward to $3 in 1866, but by 1877 the wage was back to $2 a day, only a dollar beyond the level established almost fifty years before!

Quiz Number 12

1. According to the National Football League,_____has the highest payroll.
   a) Los Angeles Rams   b) New York Jets   c) Pittsburgh Steelers   d) Philadelphia Eagles

2. In 1985 housing prices have advanced most rapidly in_____. a) Dallas b) Pittsburgh c) Atlanta d) Boston

3. In 1987, you will be able to leave_____in your will free of federal taxes.
   a) $250,000   b) $750,000   c) $400,000   d) $600,000

4. The mayor of Detroit has a salary of_____per year.
   a) $65,000   b) $79,000   c) $92,000   d) $103,000

5. Of the following,_____is *not* a franchise operation.
   a) Ugly Duckling Rent-A-Car   b) Domino's Pizza
   c) Baskin-Robbins   d) 7 Eleven

6. Recently the average nursing home cost over_____per bed to build. a) $35,000 b) $18,000 c) $12,500 d) $53,000

7. In 1983 among insured families the average amount of the policy was for_____.
   a) $28,000   b) $81,000   c) $63,000   d) $106,000

8. In 1984, of the following categories, the most new products were introduced in_____.
   a) frozen foods   b) dairy products   c) candy and gum
   d) bread, cakes, and cookies

9. Number one in worldwide airline operations is_____.
   a) Eastern   b) Northwest   c) TWA   d) Pan American

10. The net worth of the average American household is_____.
    a) $136,000   b) $23,000   c) $54,000   d) $77,000

Wages of Sin

☞ It remains a seller's market and of late women aren't selling themselves quite as cheaply as they once did. Of course all costs have risen so it is unreasonable to expect the kind of bargains once available to men in the flesh market. Needless to say, this is a highly fragmented market with deals being made continuously, often spontaneously, so keeping tabs on the price of sexual favors has always defied scientific precision. Nonetheless we are not without some historical perspective.

To the extent that price-fixed sex was possible, brothels usually served as a stabilizing force. The sex menu there would be quoted on demand and satisfaction guaranteed. Before the Great Depression, brothel charges ranged from $1 and $2 with $5 for servicing the premium carriage trade (except for godforsaken out-of-the-way locations like Fairbanks, Alaska, where nonstop business dictated whatever-the-traffic-would-bear prices). For every dollar a john handed over, a madam generally took 50¢, leaving the prostitute with the other 50¢, part of which went for expenses and at times to pimps. Prices out on the street, in the bars, and in the hotels varied but rose slowly until the depression. Around World War I they averaged $1 to $2, edged up to between $2 and $3 in the Roaring Twenties, and slipped back a bit in the 1930s to between $1 and $3 (although exclusive brothels were able to extract $5 apiece). By World War II, $5 became the national average and by the late 1960s the standard quote for straight sex was $10 a trick. Naturally the more exotic the sexual acts the higher the price. Half-and-half generally came with a $15 price tag, fellatio $20. All-night companionship could reach $100.

Recent interviews with "usually reliable sources" reveal that the New York City scene remains as lively and varied as ever with the battle for market share as intense as in the corporate world. Freelancers remain but face considerable competition and opposition from pimps determined to drive them off the street and out of business for themselves. Some call girls now wear beepers permitting more rapid response and less down time. Prices range broadly to encompass almost casual street sex to all-night affairs in plush surroundings. Low end $10 sex is reportedly still available, while call girls can start at $500 a night and head on up to $1000. In the better hotel bars the propositioning begins at $150 and will, depending upon mood and market conditions, come down to $75 for an approximately thirty-minute session. What impact concern over AIDS and herpes will have on product demand and on the price structure is not clear yet. For the moment, at least, it continues to be business as usual.

Wages of Skin

☞ Unclothed, women generally have little trouble capturing the attention of men. The publishers of *Playboy* and *Penthouse* magazines have banked millions merely by recognizing this simple fact of nature. But what have the young women gained from the unabashed display of their physical assets? *Playboy's* Playmate of the Month can expect $15,000 for hiding little if anything from the cameras. Promotional appearances will bring her an additional $300 per day. She is also in the running for Playmate of the Year, a $100,000 bonanza, with a personal appearance fee of $500 a day. *Penthouse's* Pet of the Month may cut quite a figure in front of photographers but can expect to be paid $5000, substantially less than her Playmate sister. On the other hand, the Pet of the Year has struck a pose worth $400,000 plus the considerable exposure she will enjoy during her public appearances.

Waste Profits

☞ We are, and to an extent always have been, a wasteful, profligate people. The Indians first noticed it, Europeans repeatedly commented on it, then for a time we even came to take a certain pride in it. To be wasteful simply confirmed the abundance of America. Today, however, waste makes wealth. An ever growing market exists for old discarded products and materials. This commerce has been around for quite some time. Ragpickers once plied the city streets for rags that could be converted into newsprint and roofing materials, while others collected mattresses for the value of the cotton inside. For years dentists sold the gold and silver they retrieved from tooth fillings, while used X-ray film brought returns because of the silver it contained. Today companies stand ready to buy what might appear at first glance to be useless junk. But before you go around collecting the stuff and loading up the car, get to know your prices. The following guidelines should be of some help.

It's certainly simpler to recycle paper than plant a forest. For that reason used paper commands a price. Across America, towns have taken to collecting newspapers because not only can it bring in about $10 a ton but there are substantial savings because disposal, which costs $25 a ton, is no longer necessary. Likewise computer cards should not be discarded. Expect 2¢ to 4¢ for every pound you hand in and about the same payment for computer printouts. Bond paper also has its takers. Make it white bond and you'll receive $30 a ton. For colored bond, figure $20 a ton. Mixed paper may not be worth transporting ($5 a ton).

Scrap metals hardly ever go unwanted. Copper will bring in 30¢ to 40¢ a pound, brass 25¢ to 30¢, lead 7¢ a pound, while scrap iron averages $40 a gross ton. Haul in car batteries and expect 50¢ to 70¢ for each. Load up on aluminum cans and figure on 20¢ a pound. Should you start collecting car radiators you'll walk away with 22¢ a pound for the stuff. Drag in a car or truck and count on getting $1.50 per 100 pounds of the carcass. All this may appear as slightly too crude or weighty for you. If it does, remember there are stores that will pay you for your old mink and other fur coats and others that will make you an offer for your designer clothes. Don't bother about weighing them. You won't be paid by the pound.

A Wealth of Words

☞ Almost from the beginning, Americans have been in hot pursuit of money, lusting for it, worshipping it, plotting endlessly to obtain it, working for it, dying for it. It was money they assuredly were after though they chose at times to call it something else. And so an elaborately rich and often light-hearted vocabulary emerged, created by people in need of some comic relief from the all-too-serious chase after the Almighty Dollar.

Words of foreign origin or derivation drifted in and were assimilated. Shekel, mazuma, gelt (Hebrew/Yiddish roots), cash (French), dinero (Spanish), and filthy lucre (Paul's First Epistle to Timothy) are just such imports. Then there are those words that harken back to colonial times. Wampum, that which Indians offered in exchange for goods, remains in circulation today. Buck

$ = smackeroos = money = shekel = CASH = moola = dinero = bread = WAMPUM = PILE = dough = LEGAL TENDER = buck = CABBAGE = Greenbacks = change = GRAND = scratch = filthy lucre = Simoleons = Doodle-e-squat = GREASE = PAYOLA = boodle = jack =

AURORA '85

also recalls earlier trading patterns when deerskins were prized objects of value. (Buck as distinguished from doe [or dough]?) But the buck didn't stop here, moving on to broader usage via sawbuck ($10 bill) and fast buck (quick, easy money). The fact that paper currency often bore a green tint took the terminology down some predictable paths: green, greenback, green stuff, even cabbage. Coinage encouraged additional inventiveness. "Coin of the Realm" was no mystery and with but slight explanation one could understand how "change" and "piece of change" gained acceptance.

In the understated argot of gamblers the names of minor coins often became tongue-in-cheek substitutes for considerably larger sums of money. So a nickel note translated into a $5 bill, a "small nickel" ($500) and a "big nickel" ($5000). The same folks were the principal purveyors of "grand" as representing a thousand dollars, often contracted to "G's." Nor were they averse to the term "smacker" for a dollar, originating in the sound of a silver dollar dropped upon a counter. A special nomenclature developed for money used for improper or questionable purposes. "Slush fund," "payola," "boodle," "grease"—all have decidedly dubious connotations. While "the wherewithal," "bread," "pile," and "legal tender" are readily associated with money, other terms appear as rather more whimsical, spontaneous creations, such as "simoleons," "scratch," "jack," "moola," and, yes, "doodle-e-squat." So what does all this add up to? At the very least a rich vocabulary to describe the object of what often was a single-minded pursuit.

Windfall

☞ You've just come into a fortune. A spending binge is in order. What to do first? Who has not had such daydreams? Joe Moore didn't have to wake up from his. He became a winner in the New York state lottery recently. His prize—$13.7 million. Observe now how reports indicated he handled the windfall in the days that followed.

Lotto officials hired a limousine to bring him to the official award ceremony. After considerable uncertainty as to what was expected of him now, he responded with a $5 tip to the chauffeur. For his television appearance he bought a shirt ($35) and a tie ($18). Next he indulged himself by ordering two custom-made suits from a shop on Madison Avenue ($1555 for both). Attending a birthday party for a friend's mother he brought along champagne ($27) and a box of cookies ($17). After the party it was out for drinks with a female companion (four beers at $3.50 per). A limousine home (he was beginning to enjoy this form of transportation) cost him $15 and again a $5 tip. The following day, needing stationery to write to those who had sent their congratulations, he stepped into Tiffany's and bought a box of fifty sheets for $25, a bit of an extravagance, he acknowledged. He paid for it with cash.

Not exactly the picture of wild abandon. Not yet at least. Joe did start thinking about buying an apartment in Manhattan but there is a good chance he'll just stay put in Brooklyn. He will probably remain on the job as well (as a computer consultant). If he does he will then have two jobs, the more important of which will be managing his money.

You Must Remember This

☞ The oldies but goodies often were also good and cheap. That is the not so startling conclusion of a recent New York *Post* story based on the original costs of the 1942 movie classic *Casablanca*, starring Humphrey Bogart, Ingrid Bergman, Claude Rains, and Sydney Greenstreet. Its total cost, about $878,000, was considered moderate in its day, more than *The Maltese Falcon* ($375,000) and *Knute Rockne* ($645,000) but not nearly as much as *They Died with Their Boots On* ($1.3 million). Three Hollywood producers, asked to estimate costs had *Casablanca* been shot today, produced the figure of about $25 million. Humphrey Bogart, who received $36,600 for his work in 1942, would, they estimate, easily command $4 million while Bergman, brought on board for $25,000, would be paid about $1.2 million. The camera crew, which worked back in 1942 for $11,000, would now receive $400,000 for their efforts; while a good screenwriter content then to produce the script for about $47,000 would now ask Hollywood's going rate of about $700,000. Perhaps the most startling comparison would be publicity costs. A meager $5000 went for that purpose in 1942 while today a film of some promise presently eats up a $5 million budget. Whether Bogie outwitting Nazis could outdraw Rocky outslugging Russkies is a question worthy of some reflection.

AURORA '85

1976

It would have been a shame had the United States, preoccupied by serious problems or diverted by crisis, not celebrated properly its two-hundredth birthday. No need for such concern. It couldn't have turned out better; nothing marred the occasion. And what a sight it was. Tall, majestic sailing ships from thirty-one nations clustered dramatically in New York Harbor before the Statue of Liberty, all part of the Operation Sail extravaganza. Parades and celebrations up and down the length of the land. Spectacular fireworks displays in Washington, in New York City, in Boston, and elsewhere lighting up the nights—reminding citizens that though born in fire, tested in adversity, we had come through it all and were now a success story of unparalleled dimension.

Or were we? Throughout most of the year the signals were at best mixed. On the economic front we seemed at last to be emerging from the shocks of the oil crunch and adjusting to the new realities. January turned out to be the busiest in the history of the New York Stock Exchange, while the Dow Jones Industrial Average moved up, poised for yet another assault on the magical 1000 level. Double digit inflation faded but fears of its return lay just below the surface. Auto and retail sales advanced smartly and the balance sheets recorded a record trade surplus. The GNP was on track to its next destination, $2 trillion! All this was the good news. Less welcome was the unemployment rate, which, though down, still hovered at the troublesome 8 percent level. Also of concern was the condition of some of America's banks, weakened by sizable loan losses. New York City remained in virtual bankruptcy, propped up by emergency loans of all sorts. W.T. Grant, one of the nation's largest retailers, was not as fortunate. In the end it closed its doors and went out of business, the largest retail bankruptcy in US history. This was an election year when the direction of the economy often determines the ebb and flow of political fortunes. The mixed signals suggested a close presidential contest.

Close it was. Seemingly out of nowhere the candidacy of Jimmy Carter of Georgia took hold as other Democratic contenders, Bayh, Bentsen, Harris, Sanford, Shapp, Shriver, and Jackson dropped out. In the end Carter won the nomination easily, a tribute less to his popularity and mass appeal than to his tireless, dogged campaign undertaken well in advance of the political season of 1976. Among the Republicans, incumbent Gerald Ford had all the advantages, but he still had to beat off a spirited challenge from ex-California Governor Ronald Reagan. The election campaign was the first to benefit from federal money, a total of $21.8 million for each of the principal candidates. Carter and Ford appeared in three nationally televised debates. Most observers gave Carter the edge in the debates. The public watched Carter rise in the polls, then watched as Carter's lead narrowed. But Ford never quite closed the gap. Jimmy Carter captured just slightly over 50 percent of the popular vote in an election that saw a disappointing turnout of just 53 percent of the eligible voters. An incumbent had lost, the first time that had happened since Herbert Hoover's 1932 defeat. And not since before the Civil War had a son of the Deep South occupied the highest office in the land.

Part of Carter's appeal related directly to his image as outsider distant from and skeptical of the government establishment in Washington. Events during the year tended to confirm such skepticism. A congressional committee on US Intelligence agencies and activities revealed widespread violations and illegal activities by these organizations and prompted the formation of an oversight committee to monitor such operations. FBI Director Clarence Kelly publicly admitted agency misdeeds and promised to end illegal surveillance and individual harassment. Widespread wrongdoing was not confined to government activities. During the year the Lockheed Corporation revealed systematic payments by its officers to numerous influential foreigners, bribery intended to advance Lockheed's business interests.

Medical issues and developments were in the news often during the year. In August came the announcement that scientists at the Massachusetts Institute of Technology had constructed and implanted the first complete synthetic gene. Few doubted that a threshold had been crossed and that awesome possibilities lay ahead. An expected outbreak of flu prompted the government to organize a national immunization program until apparent difficulties with the flu shots brought the effort to a halt. Mystery and death stalked some of those attending an American Legion convention in Philadelphia. In no time Legionnaire's Disease was on everyone's mind as scientific sleuths tried to uncover the cause of the outbreak. The courts were busy on the medical scene as well. Federal judges intervened to strike down restrictions on the use of Medicaid funds for abortion. The Supreme Court ended a longstanding ban and upheld the right of pharmacists to advertise drug prices. In New Jersey a court ruled that the father of Karen Ann Quinlan, long unconscious and in an irreversible coma, could allow her to die by ordering the removal of respiratory equipment. About the same time a new California law permitted terminally ill people to request the withdrawal of life-sustaining procedures. Any such action then might have to await the return of California doctors, out staging a mass slowdown in protest against huge increases in malpractice premium rates.

A slowdown also seemed to have afflicted the Equal Rights Amendment. The states of New York and New Jersey both turned it down during the year. Adding to feminist gloom, antiabortionists appeared to be back on the offensive, apparently benefiting from the statements of President Ford in favor of some restriction on abortion procedures. What feminists made of the following two stories no one could be certain. The first involved the downfall of Ohio Congressman Wayne Hays after twenty-eight years in the House, done in by a sex scandal involving his secretary. No such scandal surrounded Jimmy Carter, though he did admit in a widely publicized interview in *Playboy* Magazine that he had lusted after women in his heart. Whether this admission gained him the support of lustful men in the electorate could not be documented. What could be documented was the awesome power of the Cincinnati Reds. With a lineup that included Pete Rose, Ken Griffey, Joe Morgan, Tony Perez, Dan Driessen, George Foster, and Johnny Bench, it was hard to see how they could lose. They didn't, rolling over the New York Yankees four games to none in the World Series. Sharing honors with the Reds were such individual standouts as Bill Madlock of the Cubs who took the batting crown in the National League, George Brett of Kansas City who did the same in the American League, and the major league home-run king Mike Schmidt (with 38). But the darling of the baseball world was without doubt pitcher Mark Fidrych of Detroit. This unconventional free spirit, who insisted upon holding conversations with the baseball, apparently said the right things because in addition to his value as entertainer he compiled a lustrous win-loss record of 19–9.

The feature entertainer of all boxing continued to be Muhammad Ali, formerly Cassius Clay. He fought several times during the year although without distinction. Then on September 28 in Yankee Stadium, his first New York appearance in five years, he met and nearly met defeat at the hands of Ken Norton. Many witnesses to the bout agreed that Norton had been robbed, but then the champion ordinarily gets (maybe is even entitled to) the benefit of the doubt. Tennis fans had little reason to question the rankings of the leading players. Among the men Jimmy Connors reigned supreme though pressed at times by Bjorn Borg, Ilie Nastase, and Arthur Ashe. Chris Evert's consistency almost always wore down her opponents, though such challengers as Evonne Goolagong, Virginia Wade, and Rosemary Casals were capable at times of taking the measure. Taking the measure of the leading golfers or at least counting up their money winnings revealed the top performer to be Jack Nicklaus. Others ranked high among the moneymakers included Ben Crenshaw, Hale Irwin, Hubert Green, Al Geiberger, and J. C. Snead.

Where the stars really came out was at the Olympic Games

staged in Montreal, Canada. But more often than not the stars tended to be Russian and East German rather than American. The United States, which finished third in the unofficial point totals, did not dominate the track and field events as in the past. American entries did not win 100 or 200 meters while Cuban star Alberto Juantorena ran off with the gold in the 400 and 800 meter runs. Bruce Jenner took the coveted Decathlon championship and America continued its domination of basketball and its recent ascent in men's swimming. But the attention of American fans soon focused on the US boxing team. This spirited group of young men stole the show as Leo Randolph, Howard Davis, Ray Leonard, Michael Spinks, and Leon Spinks carried home the gold.

Gold is what some of the more successful authors struck when their books entered bestseller territory. Leon Uris was among them with his book, *Trinity*, as was Peter Benchley for *The Deep* and Joseph Wambaugh for *The Choirboys*. Hedrick Smith told us all we wanted to know about *The Russians*, and Gail Sheehy perhaps more than we were prepared to hear about middle age in *Passages*. Staying at or near the top was *Roots* by Alex Haley, an extraordinary account of the Afro-American experience. Watergate was the topic of two major books of the year, John Dean's *Blind Ambition* and Leon Jaworski's *The Right and the Power*. It also was the setting for what many judged to be the best movie of the year, *All the President's Men*, starring Robert Redford and Dustin Hoffman. Without that film the year's offerings, notably *The Omen*, *King Kong*, *Marathon Man*, and *The Bad News Bears*, were without particular distinction. On TV one didn't often expect distinction and therefore tended to settle for the comfortable and the predictable. Such were the offerings of "Happy Days," "Laverne and Shirley," "Charlie's Angels," "The Waltons," and "One Day at a Time." "M*A*S*H" had developed its own sizable following, as had "All in the Family." The sale of Six Million Dollar man dolls and accessories attested to the enormous pulling power of TV and the impact of the personalities it featured. It was hardly the real world and perhaps that's why Americans tended to turn it on for hours on end.

ODDS AND ENDS IN 1976

• The entrance fee for ABA teams wishing to enter the National Basketball Association is $3.2 million per team.

• Chris Evert, winner at Wimbledon, captures prize money of $17,000.

• National average family income is $14,000.

• In July home heating oil is at 40¢ a gallon in New York City.

• Pitching sensation Mark Fidrych of the Detroit Tigers plays for the $16,000 major league minimum.

• Citicar, the electric car built by Sebring with a top speed of 38 mph and a forty-mile range, sells for $3000.

• Plano University in Texas is auctioned off to pay teacher salaries and other expenses. The auction yields $700,000.

• Average price of a double-wide mobile home: $16,000.

• Benefit levels for the Aid to Dependent Children program range from $14.40 per recipient in Mississippi to $120 in Massachusetts.

• Muhammad Ali sends check for $100,000 to Hillside Aged Program Center in New York City to make good on his promise.

• The price of gold rises to $112 an ounce in August.

• Market price for a barrel of OPEC oil is $11.51.

• W. T. Grant bankruptcy is the second largest in history behind that of Penn Central.

• New Jersey hairstylist Eric Leek wins nation's highest lottery prize—$1776 a week for life and a guarantee of $1.8 million.

• A Gallup Poll has 44 percent in favor of reimposing price controls, 41 percent opposed, and 15 percent offering no opinion.

• A Santa Claus in New York City is paid $3 to $4 per hour.

• A thirty-second commercial on the "Sonny and Cher Show" in prime time TV costs $62,000.

• Senior partner at major New York law firm Paul Weiss, Rifkind, Wharton, and Garrison bills at $250 per hour.

• Commission on the sale of one hundred shares of AT&T (price $56) would be about $80.

• In New York, New Jersey, and Connecticut the state lotteries return about 40 percent to 45 percent of proceeds in prizes. The illegal numbers games return about 60 percent and offtrack betting 83 percent.

• New York Philharmonic musicians earn a minimum $23,000 a year.

• It cost $1.4 billion to stage the Montreal Olympics. Original estimate had been $310 million. Deficit stands at $800 million.

• January 1976 is the most spectacular month in history of the New York Stock Exchange. The Dow Jones Industrial Average rises 122 points to 975. January 30 sees a record volume of 38.5 million shares traded.

• In August the prime rate is 7 percent and six-month Treasury bills yield 5.4 percent.

• Lifetime membership in an airport VIP room costs between $225 and $300.

• Health Maintenance Organization (HMO) fees in New York per month: $29.90 for a single person, $84.10 for a family.

• All but fifteen of an experimental run of 1.5 million aluminum pennies are melted down. Four have been recovered by FBI but the estimated value of missing eleven coins is $35,000 each.

• The US Court of Appeals halts construction on the $116 million Tellico Dam in Tennessee to protect the snail darter, a small fish on the endangered species list.

• Top prices for opera tickets in Houston, $20; San Francisco, $23; New York City, $25; Paris, $30; Milan, $40; Vienna, $44.

• The FTC begins an investigation to determine whether pharmacies should be allowed to substitute less costly drugs when the substitutes are the same as the brand name drugs.

• Estimated cost of maintaining a racehorse for a year: $10,000 to $15,000.

• Number one selling doll: Cher by Mego. Suggested retail price: $6.94.

• Miami jury awards $125,000 to a woman after doctors operated on the wrong knee.

• Since 1967 fish prices have increased the most of all food items; poultry rose the least.

● Salary Levels, New York City, 1976

Advertising copy	$15,000 *per year*		Editor, experienced	$14,000 *per year*
Auto truck mechanic	to $250 *per week*		Executive secretary	$200 to $210 *per week*
Buyer, sportswear	to $29,000 *per year*		Electronic engineer	$11.50 *per hour*
Bilingual secretary	$260 *per week*		Foreman	$15,000 *per year*
Bond order clerk, Wall Street	$225 to $250 *per week*		Gal/Guy Friday	$185 *per week*
Chauffeur	$165 to $255 *per week*		MBAs	to $20,000 *per year*
Chef, cook	to $450 *per week*		Marketing research	$22,500 *per year*
Chemical engineer, experienced	to $30,000 *per year*		Optometrist	$35,000 *per year*
Clerk-typist	to $190 *per week*		Paralegal trainee	$11,000 to $13,000 *per year*
Computer programmer	$15,800 *per year*		Payroll clerk	$185 *per week*
Copywriter, experienced	to $16,500 *per year*		Pharmacist manager	to $23,000 *per year*
Corporate attorney	$35,000 to $40,000 *per year*		Physician, group practice	from $70,000 *per year*
Corporate art director	$22,000 to $25,000 *per year*		Receptionist	$140 *per week*
Corporate doctor	to $45,000 *per year*		Registered nurse, assistant director	$18,000 *per year*
Cosmetic package designer	$25,000 to $30,000 *per year*			
Dictaphone secretary	$12,000 *per year*			

● Book Prices, 1976

Wayne Dyer, *Your Erroneous Zones*	$6.95
Judith Guest, *Ordinary People*	$7.95
Clive Cussler, *Raise the Titanic*	$8.95
Leon Jaworski, *The Right and the Power*	$9.95
Leon Uris, *Trinity*	$10.95
Gail Sheehy, *Passages*	$10.95
James Michener, *Sports in America*	$12.50
John Toland, *Adolf Hitler*	$14.95

● Broadway Theater Prices, 1976

Fiddler on the Roof	$7 to $20
A Chorus Line	$7 to $15
California Suite	$6 to $15
Equus	$6 to $15
My Fair Lady	$8 to $17.50
The Wiz	$6 to $16
Same Time Next Year	$7 to $13.50

● Wages and Fringe Benefits, 1976

(per hour in manufacturing)

Sweden	$7.12
Belgium	$6.46
United States	$6.22
Canada	$6.20
West Germany	$6.19
Netherlands	$5.98
France	$4.57
Italy	$4.52
United Kingdom	$3.20
Japan	$3.10

● Foreign Currency as Percentage of US Dollar, 1976

Argentina Peso	.0085
Australian Dollar	.24
Brazil Cruzeiro	.1000
Britain Pound	1.79
Canada Dollar	1.02
France Franc	.2038
Holland Guilder	.3715
Israel Pound	.1250
Italy Lira	.0011
Japan Yen	.0034
Mexico Peso	.0801
S. Africa Rand	1.15
W. Germany Deutschmark	.3933

● Liquor Prices, 1976

Schenley vodka	$3.98 quart	Ron Rico Puerto	
John Begg scotch	$5.88 fifth	Rican rum	$5 quart
Martini & Rossi		Carstairs whiskey	$4.98 quart
gin	$4.98 fifth	Lord Calvert	
White Heather		Canadian	
scotch	$5.98 fifth	whiskey	$4.98 quart
Gilbey's gin	$5.49 quart	Chivas Regal	
Stolichnaya		scotch	$10.19 fifth
vodka	$7.24 fifth		

● Appliance Prices, 1976

	List Price	Sale
Hotpoint two-speed automatic washer	$289	$228
Welbilt 30″ gas range	$219	$178
Upright freezer 13 cubic feet	$289	$218
Admiral 16 cubic foot frost-free refrigerator	$449	$298
Sylvania 19″ color TV, portable	$378	$278

● Candy Bar Price Increase November 1976

	From	To	From	To
Peter Paul				
Mounds	1.5 ounces	1.65 ounces	15¢	20¢
Three				
Musketeers	1¹³⁄₁₆ ounces	2¹⁄₁₆ ounces	15¢	20¢

● Perfume Prices, 1976

	One Ounce
White Shoulders (Evyan)	$37.50
Halston	$100.00
Cardin	$50.00
Calandre (Paco Rabanne)	$55.00
L'air du Temps (Nina Ricci)	$55.00
Red (Geoffrey Beene)	$100.00
Rive Gauche (Yves St. Laurent)	$35.00
Norell	$100.00
Chanel No. 5	$45.00

● Record Album Prices, 1976

Streisand and Kristofferson, "A Star Is Born"	$5.99
Barry Manilow	$4.19
The Beatles, "Let It Be"	$2.99
"Stevie Wonder's Greatest Hits"	$3.49
The Jacksons	$3.99
Zero Mostel in "Fiddler on the Roof"	$4.79
Paul McCartney, "Band on the Run"	$3.99
"Threepenny Opera"	$4.99

● Houses, 1976

Price reduced—Cathedral ceiling, living room, formal dining room, three to four bedrooms, three baths, den, large kitchen with separate dinette, 40' cypress paneled playroom with fireplace, flagstone patio, large plot, walk to station.
Great Neck, New York   asking $119,500

Stunning French provincial, dramatic sunken living room, three bedrooms, handsome studio den (adjoins one bedroom), maid's room, near school, commuting.
Scarsdale, New York   low $90s

Attractive stone and stucco with terrace overlooking private garden, four bedrooms, two and a half baths, plus maid's room and bath on second floor. Center hall, modern kitchen, paneled library.
Scarsdale, New York $120s

Well maintained older home, four or five bedrooms, two and a half baths, formal dining room, family room with raised hearth, large kitchen.
Greenwich, Connecticut $129,500

● Houses, 1976

Outstanding colonial on cul de sac, near town, brick entrance hall, Good size four or five bedrooms, two and a half lovely baths, Fireplace in living room, den and many other attractive features.
    Darien, Connecticut $124,000

Year round oceanfront home, located in national seashore, high up on the dunes, lots of glass and deck, full basement, furnished three bedrooms & loft.
Wellfleet, Massachusetts
                    $107,000

● Supermarket Prices, 1976

Meat *Specials*	Per Pound
Top or bottom round roast	$1.39 to $1.49
Eye round roast	$1.79
Top sirloin steak	$1.79
Ground chuck	95¢
Ground round	$1.19
Cubed steaks	$1.59
London broil	$1.89
Shoulder steak	$1.69
Club steak	$2.99
Skirt steak	$1.39
Smoked hams	$1.59

Fish	
Fresh flounder fillet	$1.99
Fresh cod steaks	$1.49

Fowl	Per Pound
Whole chicken	45¢
Chicken cutlets	$1.79 to $1.99
Chicken breasts	95¢ to $1.15
Drumsticks	95¢
Chicken livers	89¢
Chicken thighs	89¢
Chicken legs	75¢ to 89¢
Chicken wings	69¢
Cornish hens	75¢
Swift Butterball turkey	69¢

● Fruits & Vegetable Prices, 1976

Bing cherries	69¢ per pound	Cantaloupes, extra large	69¢ each
Cultivated blueberries	59¢ per pint	Bananas	19¢ per pound

● Fruits & Vegetables Prices 1976

Watermelon	9¢ per pound	Beef franks	79¢ per pound
Nectarines	33⅓¢ per pound	Kosher franks	$1.39 per pound
Apples, Granny		Kosher corned	
Smith	33⅓¢ per pound	beef	$3.96 per pound
Juice Oranges	$1 per dozen	Kosher roast beef	$3.96 per pound
Bosc pears	33⅓¢ per pound	Kosher tongue	$3.96 per pound
Peaches	30¢ per pound	Potato salad	49¢ per pound
Mango	49¢ each	Macaroni salad	49¢ per pound
Iceberg lettuce	33⅓¢ each	Cole slaw	49¢ per pound
Potatoes, Eastern	14¢ per pound	Fresh bagels	99¢ per dozen
Potatoes,		Light & Lively	30¢ for eight
California long		yogurt	ounces
white	16¢ per pound	Skim milk	39¢ per quart
Green peppers	39¢ per pound	Florida citrus	
Red onions	49¢ per pound	orange juice	29¢ per quart
Green squash	19¢ per pound	Apple juice	69¢ per half
Tomatoes, slicing	59¢ per pound		gallon
Pascal celery	39¢ each	Hawaiian Punch	69¢ per half
Frozen peas and	33⅓¢ for a ten-		gallon
carrots	ounce package	Tetley tea bags	$1.07 for 100
Frozen corn on	79¢ for twelve		bags
the cob	ounces	Frankfurter rolls	89¢ for twenty-four
Brie cheese	$2.98 per pound	White bread	33⅓¢ for twenty-
Skandor cheese	$1.78 per pound		ounce loaf
Switzerland		Del Monte	53¢ for fifteen
Swiss cheese	$4 per pound	sardines	ounces
Domestic Swiss		Chinook salmon	$1.19 for seven
cheese	$1.98 per pound		and three-
Dorman's			quarters ounces
Muenster	59¢ for six	Bumble Bee	$1.59 for seven
slices	ounces	salmon	and three-
Kraft American	99¢ for twelve		quarter ounces
slices	ounces	Green beans,	$1 for six
Breakstone		French style	fifteen-ounce cans
cottage cheese	65¢ per pound	Fruit cocktail	$1 for three
Parkay margarine	59¢ per pound		one-pound cans
Turkey breast	$3 per pound	Sacramento	22¢ for eighteen-
Chicken roll	$1.98 per pound	tomato juice	ounce can

Peter Pan peanut butter	89¢ for eighteen-ounce jar
Bartlett pears	55¢ for twenty-ounce can
Heinz beans	88¢ for three one-pound cans
Chunk light tuna	49¢ for a six-and-one-half-ounce can

Fig Newtons	75¢ per pound
Burry's Mr. Chips	69¢ for twelve ounces
Apple Pie, Jane Parker (22 ounces)	59¢ each
Coffee	$2.16 per pound

● Unemployment Insurance Benefits, 1976

(per week)

Alabama	$66.50
Alaska	$81.82
Illinois	$91.64
Michigan	$87.82
Mississippi	$50.81
New York	$73.52
Ohio	$84.60
Wyoming	$71.89
National average	$75.16

● Total Currency in Circulation, 1976

denomination	billion
$1	$2.7
$5	$3.6
$10	$10.3
$20	$28.7
$50	$8.4
$100	$24.7
Total coins	$9.2

● Most Expensive US Cities, 1976

Houston
New York
Boston
Baltimore
Philadelphia
Minneapolis
Scranton
San Diego

● Most Heavily Taxed States, 1976

(per capita)

Hawaii	$665
Alaska	$576
Minnesota	$515
New York	$493
Wisconsin	$464
New Mexico	$452

● College Tuition, 1976

Amherst	$3725
Boston U.	$3580
Duke	$3230
Georgia	$555 Georgia resident
	$1506 out-of-state
	resident
Harvard	$3740
Idaho	$400 Idaho resident
	$1400 out-of-state
	resident
University of	$3300
Miami	
Notre Dame	$2982
Ohio State	$810 Ohio resident
	$1860 out-of-state
	resident
Pennsylvania	$1095
State	Pennsylvania resident
	$2295 out-of-state
	resident
Princeton	$4400
Rutgers	$928 New Jersey resident
	$1288 out-of-state resident
Stanford	$4275
Virginia	$465 Virginia resident
	$1465 out-of-state
	resident
Yale	$4400
Average, private	$4568
university	
Average, public	$2790
university	

● Governors' Salaries, 1976

New York	$85,000
Texas	$66,800
Pennsylvania	$60,000
Alaska	$50,000
Mississippi	$43,000
Delaware	$35,000
Idaho	$30,000
Alabama	$28,955
South Dakota	$27,500
Maryland	$25,000
Arkansas	$10,000

● Money Highlights, 1976

Purchasing power of the dollar:
    1967 = 100
    1976 = .546

Inflation from June 1975 to June 1976:
    5.91 percent

Average paycheck:
    $175 per week

Social Security:
    .9 percent on first $15,300

Gross US Debt:
    $620 billion or
    $2893 per person

Per Capita Personal Income:
    US average: $6441

● Corporate Revenues, 1976

Exxon	$47 *billion*
General Motors	$35 *billion*
AT&T	$28 *billion*
Texaco	$24.5 *billion*
Ford	$24 *billion*
Mobil	$22 *billion*
Standard Oil, California	$17.5 *billion*
Gulf Oil	$15.8 *billion*
IBM	$14.4 *billion*
Sears, Roebuck	$13.6 *billion*

● Salaries of Federal Officials, 1976

President	$200,000
Vice-President	$65,625
Cabinet	$63,000
Chief Justice	$65,600
Associate Justice	$63,000

Bonus Quiz Number 1

1. Messengers on bicycles ordinarily make upward of_____a week in New York City.
   a) $150   b) $225   c) $300   d) $475

2. Highest selling prices for existing houses will be found in_____.
   a) Florida   b) New York   c) California   d) Arizona

3. The cost of producing a six-minute cartoon today will be approximately_____.
   a) $800,000   b) $75,000   c) $520,000   d) $200.00

4. ABC charged_____for a thirty-second spot during its broadcast of the 1984 Olympics.
   a) $230,000   b) $175,000   c) $310,000   d) $110,000

5. A medium-priced car quoted in New York City for $7600 will cost about_____in Tel Aviv, Israel.
   a) $10,200   b) $19,600   c) $5,200   d) $13,100

6. In 1983 life insurance companies in the United States dispensed_____of their monies in benefit payments.
   a) 76 percent b) 65 percent c) 87 percent d) 51 percent

7. In 1983 income from premium payments represented_____ of total income of US life insurance companies.
   a) 69 percent b) 91 percent c) 47 percent d) 82 percent

8. In 1984 charitable contributions by individuals totaled_____billion.
   a) 12.8   b) 31   c) 61.5   d) 96

9. Workers in manufacturing receive the highest wages in ____.
   a) Canada   b) West Germany   c) Italy   d) France

10. The 1986 list price for Chevrolet Corvette is_____.
    a) $18,990   b) $34,220   c) $22,500   d) $27,027

Answers: 1) c; 2) c; 3) d; 4) a; 5) b; 6) d; 7) a; 8) c; 9) a; 10) d.

Bonus Quiz Number 2

1. As paid consultant to the Library of Congress Gwendolyn Brooks will be paid_____for the year.
   a) $18,500   b) $35,000   c) $50,000   d) $62,500

2. Estimates have it that we've lost or lost track of_____ worth of stocks and bonds over the years.
   a) $2.1 billion b) $900 to $950 million c) $15 billion d) $22 billio

3. Racing driver_____leads the pack currently in career winnings.
   a) Al Unser, Jr.   b) Bobby Allison   c) Cale Yarborough
   d) Darrel Waldrip

4. The average graduate of Cornell Medical School owes_____.
   a) $40,000   b) $70,000   c) $18,000   d) $95,000

5. The average dental school graduate owes_____.
   a) $18,000   b) $38,000   c) $28,000   d) $52,000

6. Of the states listed,_____pays its teachers more on the average. a) Ohio b) Maryland c) Connecticut d) Rhode Island

7. The state that pays its teachers the lowest average salaries is_____.
   a) Arkansas   b) South Dakota   c) Alabama   d) Utah

8. In October 1985 a woman depositing twenty-three one-hundred-dollar bills at a drive-in bank counter in Boulder, Colorado, saw a gust of wind blow them away. Of the twenty-three,_____were recovered or returned.
   a) all   b) none   c) twelve   d) twenty

9. According to the American Bar Association lawyers in private practice average_____a year.
   a) $61,000   b) $32,000   c) $82,000   d) $43,000

10. In 1983 the San Diego Chargers were sold for_____million.
    a) 94,000   b) 46   c) 34   d) 72

☞ *Answers:* 1) b; 2) c; 3) d; 4) a; 5) c; 6) d; 7) b; 8) d; 9) a; 10) d.

Bonus Quiz Number 3

1. In 1941 the total cost of the Mount Rushmore monument in South Dakota was_____.
   a) $13.2 million b) $989,000 c) $24.3 million d) $4.1 million

2. During the height of the California Gold Rush in 1849 the average miner made_____per day.
   a) $16 b) $412 c) $72 d) $150

3. For the 1985/86 academic year,_____was the most expensive college.
   a) Bennington b) Columbia c) Vanderbilt d) Notre Dame

4. Average player salaries are highest in which professional sport?
   a) football   b) baseball   c) basketball   d) hockey

5. The percentage of mothers with children under 6 who worked in 1984 was_____.
   a) 39 percent b) 45 percent c) 52 percent d) 62.6 percent

6. In 1984_____banks failed, the highest number since 1937.
   a) 43   b) 79   c) 204   d) 162

7. In 1985, of the cities listed,_____was the least expensive to live in.
   a) New York   b) London   c) Rome   d) Tokyo

8. Over a lifetime of driving a series of new compact cars, your major expense will be_____.
   a) depreciation b) maintenance c) gas and oil d) insurance

9. In 1984 $241.6 million represented the_____for AT&T.
   a) taxes paid by   b) losses of   c) investment tax credit of   d) tax refund to

10. A video cassette selling 100,000 units merits a_____award.
    a) gold   b) silver   c) platinum   d) diamond

Bonus Quiz Number 4

1. Over the last ten years the best rate of return was from_____.
   a) diamonds   b) stamps   c) US coins   d) stocks

2. The Rolls-Royce top-of-the-line Silver Spur limousine costs_____.
   a) $105,000   b) $225,000   c) $145,000   d) $195,000

3. You can buy a full-size cardboard human skeleton that is anatomically accurate and has good mechanical features for_____.
   a) $50   b) $325   c) $175   d) $225

4. There were_____NFL teams that lost money in the 1984/85 football season.   a) 0   b) 5   c) 2   d) 9

5. The average salary in the NFL in the 1985/86 season is_____.
   a) $95,000   b) $145,000   c) $210,000   d) $190,000

6. The average 1984 compensation, including salary, bonuses, and stock options for the chief executive in the nation's twenty-fifth largest companies was_____.
   a) $620,000 b) $1.3 million c) $2.2 million d) $770,000

7. The IRS estimates tax cheaters number_____of all taxpayers.
   a) 7 percent b) 31 percent c) 12 percent d) 19 percent

8. The top fee the Metropolitan Opera in New York City pays for a soloist for each performance is_____.
   a) $8000   b) $12,500   c) $5000   d) $17,500

9. In 1985 the winner of the world championship of "Monopoly" won_____top prize.
   a) $100,000   b) $5000   c) $15,000   d) $50,000

10. Late in 1985 the highest paid player in baseball was said to be_____.
    a) Reggie Jackson   b) Eddie Murray   c) Dave Winfield
    d) George Foster

☞ *Answers:* 1) c; 2) d; 3) a; 4) b; 5) d; 6) b; 7) d; 8) d; 9) a; 10) b.

Bonus Quiz Number 5

1. The average transaction charged on stolen VISA cards is_____.
   a) $125   b) $650   c) $1060   d) $1575

2. The maximum award you can receive for turning in a tax evader is_____.
   a) $5000   b) $10,000   c) 0   d) $50,000

3. The entry fee for the Kentucky Derby in 1985 was
   a) $10,000   b) $8500   c) $20,000   d) $500

4. Production costs for the Broadway show *La Cage aux Folles* amounted to_____.
   a) $2 million b) $12.2 million c) $5 million d) $10 million

5. The British pay_____per episode of "Dallas."
   a) $60,000   b) $500,000   c) $210,000   d) $1 million

6. _____holds the all time one-week Broadway box office sales record.
   a) *My Fair Lady* b) *Oklahoma!* c) *The King and I* d) *Hair*

7. Nationwide average yearly salary for on-air television talent is_____.
   a) $65,000   b) $20,000   c) $37,000   d) $76,000

8. In 1983 the overwhelming number of daily newspapers were selling for_____per copy.
   a) 20¢   b) 25¢   c) 15¢   d) 30¢

9. It costs_____to introduce color into a 1930s Shirley Temple black-and-white movie.
   a) $110,000 b) $1.3 million c) $300,000 d) $750,000

10. Pepsi gave Michael Jackson and his family the largest single celebrity fee ever. It was_____.
    a) $2 million b) $12 million c) $3.5 million d) $5 million

Bonus Quiz Number 6

1. In July 1984 the average price of a foreign-built car sold in the United States was_____.
   a) $8500   b) $10,199   c) $12,138   d) $7469

2. In 1949 Marilyn Monroe was paid_____for posing in the nude.
   a) $250   b) $500   c) $150   d) $50

3. Today it costs_____to produce each print (copy) of a full-length motion picture.
   a) $1300   b) $89   c) $2500   d) $750

4. In 1910 tuition per year at Columbia University was_____.
   a) $250   b) $600   c) $1100   d) $1800

5. Richard Nixon's signature is currently worth about_____.
   a) $50   b) $80   c) $180   d) $450

6. A milk cow today costs about_____.
   a) $900   b) $2250   c) $375   d) $1575

7. On the lecture circuit Walter Cronkite may get up to_____ per appearance.
   a) $40,000   b) $7500   c) $12,500   d) $20,000

8. The chemical elements in the human body are worth_____.
   a) $22.14   b) $8.37   c) $4.52   d) $30.52

9. Of the 163.2 billion manufacturers' coupons distributed in 1984,_____were redeemed.
   a) 0.3 percent   b) 12.8 percent   c) 4 percent   d) 17 percent

10. In 1984, the most money gambled legally was in_____.
    a) horse racing   b) dog racing   c) lotteries   d) slot machines

Answers: 1) c; 2) d; 3) a; 4) a; 5) a; 6) a; 7) a; 8) a; 9) b; 10) d.

Bonus Quiz Number 7

1. In 1984 the forty-three new members of the House of Representatives spent an average of _____ on their campaigns.
   a) $459,000 b) $1.2 million c) $127,000 d) $822,000

2. Tunica County, Mississippi, presently has the highest poverty rate in the US with a rate of _____ percent.
   a) 52.9 b) 28.2 c) 19.6 d) 38.1

3. About _____ of US households don't have checking accounts.
   a) 12 percent b) 30 percent c) 20 percent d) 7 percent

4. The annual budget of the IRS is approximately _____.
   a) $1.2 billion b) $872 million c) $6 billion d) $9.8 billion

5. A master's degree can be bought from a diploma mill for about _____.
   a) $1250 b) $2100 c) $3500 d) $4200

6. The last time a first-class stamp cost 5¢ was in _____.
   a) 1955 b) 1969 c) 1963 d) 1959

7. David Stockman reportedly received _____ for a book relating his experiences in government.
   a) $750,000 b) $520,000 c) $1.2 million d) $2 million

8. In a recent survey of 700 typical millionaires _____ inherited a substantial portion of their wealth.
   a) 5 percent b) 51 percent c) 37 percent d) 20 percent

9. Recent reports indicate that the car most likely to be stolen is a _____.
   a) Buick Riviera b) Cadillac Eldorado c) Porsche 911
   d) Mazda RX-7

10. At Harvard's 1985 graduation _____ of the 1,500 seniors were economics majors.
    a) 225 b) 568 c) 95 d) 425

Bonus Quiz Number 8

1. According to the IRS _____ billion will be the difference between the taxes we should be paying and what the government will receive in 1986.
   a) 220   b) 45   c) 90   d) 175

2. The highest salary earned by Honus Wagner, eight-time batting champion of the National League, was _____.
   a) $10,000   b) $6500   c) $18,000   d) $21,000

3. Edward Koch's salary as mayor of New York City is _____.
   a) $85,000   b) $210,000   c) $110,000   d) $145,000

4. A year's subscription to *Pravda* costs $34.50. The new English language version of this Russian newspaper will cost _____ annually. a) $75   b) $125   c) $110   d) $630

5. The highest salary Ted Williams ever made in baseball was _____.
   a) $85,000   b) $105,000   c) $70,000   d) $125,000

6. US cabinet officers are paid _____ a year.
   a) $86,200   b) $62,500   c) $95,000   d) $71,500

7. Financial planners ordinarily assign about _____ of the family budget for debt payments.
   a) 10 percent b) 20 percent c) 15 percent d) 6 percent

8. The most dollar volume is generated by the _____ gasoline credit card?   a) Gulf   b) Texaco   c) Shell   d) Amoco

9. Late in 1985 _____ was removed from the list of Dow Jones industrials.
   a) Colgate Palmolive b) Boeing c) American Brands d) Polaroid

10. Together, an entertainment star's general manager, booking agent, and business manager will receive approximately _____ of the total earning.
    a) 10 percent b) 15 percent c) 21 percent d) 30 percent

☞ *Answers:* 1) c; 2) a; 3) a; 4) d; 5) d; 6) a; 7) a; 8) c; 9) c; 10) d.

Index

Dallas, 154
Dalton School, tuition, 190
Dartmouth College student aid, 163
Days Inn franchise, 84
DC comics, ad rates, 86
Deerfield Academy, tuition, 189
Deer Hunter, The, 49
Deodorant sales, 2
Depression, 53
Devil's Bag, 166
DiMaggio, Joe, 138
Diplomas, bogus, 58–59
Disposable diapers, sales, 2, 53–54
Doctorow, E.L., 21
Doctors
 charges, 1846, 56
 current income, 57
 malpractice, 95–98
Dog World, ad rates, 86
Doktor Pet franchise, 84
Dollar, purchasing power, 219
Dow Jones Average, 75, 211
Dunne, Irene, 66
Dynasty, 154

Ebony, ad rates, 86
Educational expenditures, 1926, 32
Elaine Powers franchise, 84
Elephant, Asian, cost of, 6
Elk antlers, 150
Embezzlement, 66
Entertainment prices
 1926, 35
 1936, 68, 73
 1946, 106, 108
 1966, 180
Entertainers, expenses, 12–13
Evert, Chris, 210
Extras (movies), 79–80

Facial tissues, sales, 2

Fairbanks, Douglas, 30
Falcon Crest, 154
Fall Guy, The, 153
Family Ties, 153
Fidrych, Mark, 210
Federal Art Project, 6–7
Ferraro, Geraldine, 183
Final Cut, 49
Firehouse Magazine, ad rate, 86
Fisher, Mel, 14, 15
Food prices
 1926, 32
 1936, 69, 70, 72
 1946, 110
 1956, 143
 1976, 216–17
Fools Die (Puzo), 20
Football
 franchises, cost of, 1936, 66
 receipts, bowl games, 1946, 107
Forbes Magazine, 17
 "400," 82–83
Ford, Gerald, 159, 183
Foundation assets, 1966, 178
Franchising fees, 83
Friedman, Milton, 183
Fruits, dried, sales of, 2
Funeral charges, 66
Fur coats
 1926, 34
 1946, 108
Furniture prices, 1926, 34

Galah bird, 150
Galbraith, John, 183
Garvey, Steve, contract terms, 92
Gasoline prices, 1926, 31
GI bill benefits, 106
Giraffes, cost of, 6
Gnus, cost of, 6